KING OF THE ROAD

BOB TUCK

Published by Bob Tuck
Low Worsall, Yarm,
Cleveland, England TS15 9QA

ISBN 0 9521938 4 1

First Published 1999

copyright 1999 Bob Tuck

Other books by Bob Tuck

Moving Mountains
Mountain Movers
Mammoth Trucks
Hauling Heavyweights
The Supertrucks of Scammell
*Move It (compendium of Moving Mountains
and Mountain Movers)*
Carrying Cargo
Classic Hauliers
Robsons
Classic Hauliers 2
The Golden Days of Heavy Haulage
A Road Transport Heritage
A Road Transport Heritage Vol II
A Road Transport Heritage Vol III
100 Years of Heavy Haulage
Trucks (Reprint of Mammoth Trucks)

Printed in Great Britain by
The Amadeus Press Ltd
Huddersfield,
West Yorkshire

Typesetting by Highlight Type Bureau Ltd
Bradford, West Yorkshire

Book design by
Sylbert Productions
Pavey Ark.

ACKNOWLEDGEMENTS

The first mention must go to my wife Sylvia who
somehow manages to put up with my moods of
depression and anxiety. Amongst the many jobs
she does without complaint is proof reading all
my material, although she once remarked that this
section of the book is getting longer and longer. It
may be true but it's also true that I need to rely on
many people to help me put a book together.

I do at times forget to mention some. Phil Moth
recently took me to task for not recognising his
assistance in the many past volumes. Sorry Phil,
his talent to produce quality photographic prints
from the most ancient pieces of negative still
amazes me. He can also do it for you - as he now
does the job full time.

I also seem to take for granted all the help given
by the team from Amadeus. The artistic talents of
Robert Charlesworth in particular are worth a
mention for this volume.

Throughout the book I have tried to mention
either the source of the material or the
photographer in the respective captions but to
emphasize, I must thank the following who have
generously allowed me to use their material: Terry
Agland, Roger Austin, Gordon Baron, Dick Bass,
Bill Beadnell, Graham Booth, Mick Bradley,
Chris Brailsford, Brian Burgess, Andrew Burton,
Jimmy Campbell, Kevin Cobb, John Curwen,
Dick Denby, Arthur Duckett, Fred Dunn, Ken
Durston, Edwin Elliott, Joe Elliott, John Frost,
Tommy Gibb, Alan Graham, Dennis Harris, Jack
Hill, Ian Holliday, Carl Jarman, Roger Kenny, Jack
Kimp, Bill Kirsop, Malcolm Ladd, Dave Lee,
Peter Lee, Ron Lucas, Brian Maloney, Alan
Martin, Steve Mayle, Geoff Meek, Gary Miller,
Geoff Milne, Alf Moore, Roger Mortimore, Arthur
Phillips, Bill Reid, Tom Riding, Stuart Ritchie,
Rick Roberton, Fred Robinson, Paul Starkey, Tom
Shanks, Rod Spratley, John Thomas, and Mark
Walker.

Those who've also helped to make the text more
interesting with snippets of information include:
Roy Atkinson, Derek Bailey, Derrick Bowen, Tony
Brown, Tyson and Andrew Burridge, Eddie Crozier,
John Davison, Len Dobie, Chris Gardner, Tony
Knowles, Glynne Perry, Peter Searson, Dennis
Smith, Peter Slade, Peter Sunter and Jason Yates.
The thoughts of Frank Strange are always
appreciated while I mustn't forget to mention
Glynne Rees who's ability to recall so much detail is
amazing - for one with such a young looking face.

A special thanks both to Paul Hancox and Dave
Weston. Their continued help with so many of my
projects is very much appreciated. Especially
when they could both be producing books under
their own name.

CONTENTS

Front Cover

There are certainly stronger heavy haulage tractor units than Watkinsons Foden 8x4 80 tonner but there's few more versatile ones. Kitted out with a 48 tonne/metre Effer crane, 'Sapphire' as it's named, has shown it's true potential on numerous windfarm construction projects in all parts of the UK. While many vehicles find it hard enough working on tarmac'd roads, driver Terry O'Hara and his eight legger are more at home on rutted tracks on the sides of mountains. The combination is pictured during 1997 on the Novar Estate, near Evanton, about 15 miles north of Inverness. The load is a 32 tonne nacelle which makes up the generating heart of an individual wind turbine. The Foden was modified for this testing line of work by Drinkwaters of Leyland while the original 14 litre Cummins 380 engine was uprated to produce an extra 45bhp.

Front and rear montages

I make no excuse for indulging in the coverage of yet more eight wheelers at the start and end of this book. The camera of Joe Donaldson provides much of the material together with contributions from Roger Kenny, Ben Ford, Bill Kirsop and even myself. As a young transport enthusiast growing up in the late 1950s and early '60s, the sight and sound of an eight wheeler brought pleasure to the day. I class myself as fortunate in being able to spend my early years in the town of Consett, County Durham, when the local steel works proved to be a magnet for eight leggers from all parts of the country. Sadly, like those steel works, those days are long gone and the younger generation of transport enthusiast may never see the like again.

Rear Cover

One of the most famous (and most photographed) Macks in the UK must be Chris Miller's 'Bonzo Bear'. While Chris might cringe when he reads another reference to Dinorwic, it's a fact that assisting in the building of this specialist North Wales power station reaped tremendous praise for this head turning six wheeler - although it was certainly helped by the efforts of the hard working Miller team (including Dave Bunting who took this shot). When Chris came out of heavy haulage, the Mack was sold on to David Crouch Recovery of Leicestershire. After using it for some time, David sold it to Coastal Excavations of Preston.

C&B Haulage of Newbury have operated many F88s in the past although FJO 515S wasn't one of them. New in 1977, the 4x2 290 powered unit was bought by C&B sub contractor Paul Perris in 1993 from Swindon based owner driver Alan James. Restored to as new condition, Paul used it for more than four years on UK long distance general haulage before selling it for preservation to Richard Payne of Wyboston in Bedfordshire. Being an F88 nut, Paul subsequently bought another of these classic Volvos - this one being a more versatile six wheeled unit VTA 872S.

The seventh Renault Magnum to come into the UK was bought by Robin & Lily Borthwick of Stirling. In just less than five years, the 380bhp 'Big, Blue and Beautiful' did more than 800,000kms on traction work usually for operators like Curries of Dumfries. It's not surprising that when Robin did fancy a new vehicle then another Magnum, P740 TGB, took its place. However, unlike the distinctive livery applied by Robin Johnstone to J654 FSU, the bigger 420 Magnum - bearing the name 'Lily' - which the Borthwicks operate in 1999 was in the standard colours of Eddie Stobart.

Title Page

To me, the Mark III tin front AEC Mammoth Major eight wheeler of the late 1950s had a classic look which hasn't been matched. The vehicle found favour with many operators as diverse as the fuel concern of Shell Mex-BP Ltd, the Tate & Lyle subsidiary of Silver Roadways and London Brick as well as independents like Sam Anderson. Based at Newhouse near Motherwell, Sam Anderson began in haulage during the second World War with two vehicles working inside the Royal Ordnance Factory at Bishopton. On nationalisation he had 30 vehicles taken over but by using the arrangement of 'C' hiring licences, Andersons kept themselves in haulage. By 1957, the company was operating more than 100 vehicles of which 47 eight wheelers were used on regular trunk services to Birmingham, Manchester and London. When buying new AECs, Andersons fitted their own bodies and cabs which incorporated strengthened roofs to support the sheet racks. Those in shot without the racks are believed to be cabs of either Homalloy or Duramin build. Sam always reckoned that by fitting larger 40x8 tyres, he could increase the AEC's top speed to 38mph although when he bought the ex Allison eight wheelers GCW 46 and GCW 98, they had six speed boxes and a capability of 44mph.

Introduction Page

You ask many people what they think about when you say the words 'King of the Road' and they'll answer: 'The Scammell Contractor'. Whether it's in crew cab or small cab version, the 240 tonner Scammells were in a class of their own. I make no excuses for featuring this much photographed GEC Larne load again as the sight of the ex Siddle Cook 6x4 heading up the much travelled 'Betsy' – TRL 924H – during 1977 is certainly special. The next time these two Scammells got together was in that haven of many mature Scammells – Peter Court's quarry near Banbury. Terry Hoyle was to subsequently restore the ex Cooky Scammell during the early 1990s into better than new condition but when he was obliged to sell it, the big Contractor was bought by ALE who put it back to work.

KING OF THE ROAD

AUTHOR'S INTRODUCTION

As some of you may be aware, I've been planning this particular book for over 10 years. Finalizing the contents never mind the research has seemed to have taken far too much time and it's upsetting to me that Frank Boydon, for one, will never be able to read about his input.

This book is a personal selection of what I've described as Classic Lorries of Yesteryear and Super Trucks of Today. The terminology is probably how an enthusiast would describe the contents as in essence that's what I am.

I suppose everyone would have their own choice of vehicles for a book of this nature. I mentioned to a friend that I was featuring the Guy Invincible and he almost had hysterics: 'You could never call that King of the Road,' he said but to me, the Invincible was something special and that's why it's included along with the other specific vehicles.

The theme which I've taken is that at every point in time, there's always been one lorry / wagon / truck which has stood out above the rest. In earlier times the wagon and drag was the leader but when the eight wheeled rigid arrived, this took up the top status.

I suppose the 1970s was the most exciting of times. The F88, the Crusader, the Marathon, and the Transcontinental impressed both here and abroad while anything with a Mack badge on the front was always going to be a Classic. Selecting the Atkinson Borderer as well from this time slot may not bring total agreement, but this book, I stress, is a personal choice.

My only hope is that I'll be around long enough in the 21st Century to see the arrival of even more vehicles which would gain this special status.

Pavey Ark, Low Worsall,
Yarm, North Yorkshire.
August 1999

WAGON AND DRAGS

Haulage really began with the forerunner to the wagon and trailer. Man power may have been replaced by the horse or other form of animal, but the concept of dragging the load behind was continued into the mechanised age with the steam traction engine.

The arrival of the vehicle powered by the internal combustion engine developed the idea that goods could be carried on the vehicle rather than on a trailer behind. But for heavier weights, the wagon & drags always seemed a better combination. Right up until 1964, these outfits could gross 32 tons which was well ahead of the 24 tons maximum then in force of either rigid eight wheelers or four axled artics. Yes, so far as status went, the wagon and drags were well ahead.

There were of course drawbacks. For years their speed limit was always 10mph behind conventional HGVs and there was a long time requirement to carry an attendant or mate. Some outfits of old were fitted with a trailer brake that the mate operated by a hand lever but with the advent of better brakes which were piped through to the trailer, the mate had nothing to do once the vehicle was in motion. The job as a mate however, proved to be a stepping stone for many (including me) towards being a driver (although I didn't make it).

Even though the status of wagon & drags has been eroded, generally these outfits are still longer than their conventional artic counterparts. While in some parts of the world, they're a lot longer than you can imagine.

John Fowler & Co set up in the production of steam ploughing engines & machinery at Leeds around 1880 and was to acquire a reputation of second to none with the heaviest class of road locomotive. The firm was also to enjoy great success in the world wide, export market. The versatility of operating a haulage tractor was they could handle all manner of trailers. Pictured in Reading, Berkshire during 1909 is the then new Fowler no. 11441 belonging to Chas Openshaw of Reading which is hauling probably the contents, of one large stately home in three furniture pantechnicons on behalf of Heelas, Sons & Co Ltd also of Reading. Prior to 1921, road locomotives weren't allocated registration marks.

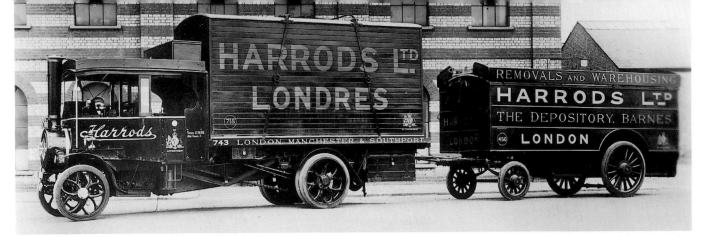

Harrods operated about a dozen Foden 5 ton steam wagons during the 1920s specifically for household removals. The pictured Foden, however, is the 6 tonner YE 7695 (maker's no.12552) which was new in March 1927. As the demountable container suggests, Harrods did have a shop in Paris at this time. The back drop is of their famous depositry. Situated near Hammersmith Bridge at Barnes, the location was a regular marker in the commentary of the annual boat race between Cambridge and Oxford universities.

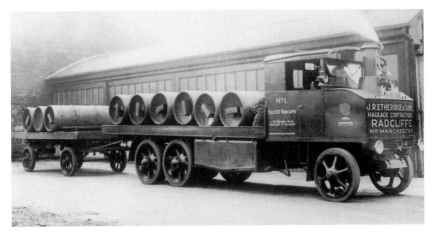

The Yorkshire Patent Steam Wagon Co had their main office and works at Hunslet, Leeds and naturally picked up a lot of their custom in the northern part of England. This WJ type six wheeler TE 5690 (maker's no. 2150) in the livery of J R Etheridge was new in 1928. The Yorkshire was perhaps best known in the steam world for the way they mounted their boiler transversely across the vehicle - rather than in line. Yorkshire were able to make the transition to diesel powered vehicles and even built a Gardner powered eight wheeler in 1936 but production of goods carrying vehicles was not sustained.

The Callow Rock Lime Company's DG4 Sentinel wagon and trailer YD 6587 (maker's no.8784) was new in March 1933. Both parts of the outfit were fitted with revolving floors to discharge the payload area. The pictured driver is Edward Flinders with mate Charlie Day. One recollection of Ken Durston (who traced the photograph) is this outfit regularly ran to Bristol with lime and backloaded with coal - to burn in the lime kilns. About half a mile before the Sentinel reached the A38 lights at Churchill, Charlie got out and walked to the junction where he stopped all the traffic. When clear, Edward set the Sentinel away and a clean run through the junction was the only way it could climb the next hill - although obviously Charlie had to climb it on foot. It's believed this Sentinel has been preserved and currently resides in Essex.

Strange as it may seem, Scammell had been in production for seven years before producing their first rigid four wheelers as their famous articulated six and eight wheeled outfits had grabbed the headlines - and the order book. The six and eight ton capacity four wheelers had a striking look to them and when coupled to a matching drawbar trailer would have been a head turning combination. Dating from 1931, this outfit sports Scammell built bodies, electric lights but still a hand operated trumpet horn. Its petrol engine drove to a four speed gearbox and an overhead worm drive rear axle. Thomas Allen operated this contract liveried outfit from their depot in Great Hermitage Street, Wapping. Guinness was shipped over from Ireland in 54 gallon capacity casks and bottled in this country until the Park Royal brewery was opened in 1936.

Followers of Gibb's of Fraserburgh will be aware that the company never operated wagon and drags although this incident in February 1955 appears to disprove this. HSA 388 was the Leyland Comet ECO2/4R (new in September '52) which is on its side some three miles south of Stonehaven on the old A90 road. Driver James Weir had miscalculated where the edge of the road was hidden in the snow but fortunately damage was slight. Jimmy is seen on the left of shot while the other figures are (left to right) mechanic Charlie Christie; Tommy Gibson and Tommy Gibbs on top of the AEC while Iain Milne then Iain Clark are sheeting down the load of transhipped seed oats. Iain Clark was the driver of the Thornycroft behind the AEC Monarch HAV 838 and was something of a comedian. His party trick if he had a passenger travelling with him was to pull off the Thorny's steering wheel - as he was driving along - and offer it across the cab with the remark: 'Do you want to drive.'

The status of the wagon & drag is clearly illustrated in this Malcolm Ladd supplied photograph which shows the fleet of St Helens based Davies & Brownlow in 1937. Even though the petrol engined Scammell dates from the early '30s and is a lot older than the Leylands behind, it's deemed to be the fleet leader in a situation like this. The Scammell is something of a rarity in that it also incorporates a single tyred, third axle conversion to increase its original 8 ton capacity. The protracted research of Malcolm Wilford reveals the Leyland Beavers in this shot are DJ 6561 and 6562 (both new in July 1935), DJ 6734 (new in December '35), DJ 6806 (new January '36) and DJ 7411 new in February 1937.

To the folk who lived in Consett, County Durham during the 1950s (including myself) the local 'King of the Road' was Consett Iron Company's fleet of 13 specially built AEC Mandator ballast box tractors that hauled Crane drawbar trailers. Fleet numbers 1-8 had consecutive registrations JUP 926-933, No. 9 was KPT 951 and 10, LUP 880. The AEC drivers normally did an eight hour shift each doing two return trips to the rolling mills at Jarrow carrying billets down and running back empty. With 9.6 engine and five speed 'box, top speed for the 4x2s was 28mph although they did run at 32 tons gross train weight. Tommy Ratcliffe was driver of No.1 and he's pictured carrying a crane flight in the area of the works known as Blast Bottom. The leading figure is Peter Mantle who was head trailer fitter at the time. Other Company drivers were Harry Stobbs and Jack Hays (No.5), Billy Ramage and Joe Lee (No.7), George Thompson (No.8), Freddie Wales (No.10), Jimmy Gibbons (No.12), Matty Walton (No.13) and Jackie Turnent who crewed No.1 with Tommy. About 1960, these outfits were replaced by 24 ton gross AEC Mandator artics. Although the artics carried approximately 4 tons less payload, they didn't have the expense of carrying a trailer mate and could do 48mph. Although most of the box tractors were sold on, No.1 was kept to work internally where gross weights - with a load of ingots - could easily reach 65 tons. The CIC drivers may have missed the strength of the old tractors but they didn't miss the awful snaking motion if they ever threw the stick out (coasted in neutral) while carrying a full load of billets.

Fred Dunn started driving at Ribble Paper Mills, Winery Lane, Walton-le-Dale near Preston in 1957. His first vehicle was a pre-war Gardner 5LW powered Albion with rod brakes which Fred said wouldn't stop you in three counties. When he took the vehicle into Albion Motors in Glasgow the foreman there said the brakes were fine - provided it didn't exceed 20mph - which was no good for Fred. In '57 Ribble were running two Atky eight wheelers and trailers, an AEC four wheeler and drag plus five Leyland Tiger vans (converted bus chassis') which included the ex Southdown DUF 181. Fred soon got the 1954 UTD 943 which hauled a Crane drawbar trailer. Gardner 6LW powered (top speed 28mph) Fred recalls he often ran closer to 40 tons than his 32 tons limit. Accompanied by mate Brian Hartley, a regular night run was to London but they then had to tip and re-load (with waste paper) during the day: 'I got an extra £2 in my hand if there wasn't a day shunter and we had to do it ourselves.' In 1960 Fred got the new 298 MTE which still pulled the old Crane trailer. Although the new Atky had the Gardner 6LX-150, it never pulled like the old 6LW. One memorable double head was a winter climb up Shap: 'One of Harry Haigh's old ERF eight wheelers pulled us up there. We only managed because my trailer mate at the time, Harvey Burrows, climbed into the ERF and jammed the starting handle into the engine to pull back the fuel pump rack. There was about 6' of flame shooting out of the ERF's exhaust but it got us to the top.'

Daniel Morrison Smith first set up in haulage back in 1929 at Canderside Toll near Lanark and although he lost his fleet in nationalisation, he set up again in '54 after buying the old BRS Wishaw operation. DM Smith always specialised in long distance work with 11 Corbett's Passage being their first London office. These premises were rather small prompting the move to 49-51 Southampton Way, Camberwell and pictured here is Smiths only wagon & drag. Hauling drums of cable, the Atkinson was usually driven by Willie Miller of Larkhall. While able to carry more freight than anything else, Smiths found the outfit a handful. They much preferred the solo four wheeler - even for long distance work - an option still in use in the late 1990s.

Of the hundreds of vehicles which the Williams Brothers were to operate, WUN 57 was still rather special. Of the three brothers involved in the business, John Williams - who ran the Treuddyn depot - was apparently a big Atkinson man. Atkys didn't come much bigger than this eight wheeler and drag which is pictured with driver Glynn Williams and mate Ivor Williams. Derrick Bowen's research reveals this outfit did regular livestock hauls (three times a week) between Denbigh in North Wales and North Devon although it was also used as a pigeon transporter during the summer months. Geared down to deal with the testing Welsh hills, the Atkys top speed was only 25mph and it was also too big to get into some of the farms. In that situation, smaller vehicles would do the collections and then tranship onto WUN 57. The Williams Brothers set up in haulage during the late 1940s and their name is still in use albeit as part of the large TDG organisation.

Historically, the car transporter industry has always had a strong following for the wagon & drags. The extra length permissible to squeeze on more fee earning vehicles has often outweighed some of its early disadvantages. In the early '60s when artics could only carry five cars, the wagon and drags of Carrimore construction could usually carry nine. If you wanted to carry even more cars, then you had to head for Tamworth and make the acquaintance of the late Alastair Carter. The first Carter outfits (top) were fairly modest although Alastair always argued that the basic slopers - as they were called - could be often more productive if you were carrying cars over shorter distances. The modest outlay in cost, lack of maintenance for raising decks and the speed in which they could be loaded / unloaded, could add up to an advantage. However, his half cab specials (left and bottom) were certainly different. A combination of a change in the law allowing wider goods vehicles and the arrival of small cars like the Mini and Hillman Imp, saw Alastair come up with the idea of using the half cabs to accommodate a car alongside the driver and mate (who were sat line astern). In this form, the AEC Reliance coach chassis may not have been the easiest vehicle to drive (wrapped knuckles were a regular hazard) but the brilliance of Mr Carter took some beating. In total, Alastair built something like 800 trailers before selling out Carveyor Ltd to Crane Fruehauf in November 1973.

It took a change of the law in 1965 to curb some of the strange Carter practices and throughout the 1970s, there was little major change in the car transporting industry. While operators could only gaze on in envy at practices adopted in some far reaching parts of our Colonies (top) it took the involvement of Alan Cooper from Tolemans with the French trailer building concern of Lohr to produce an outfit which put the car carrying industry on its head. These strange looking outfits of very small drawing units and extra long drawbar trailers (middle) may now be common place but their requirement has become paramount as cars have generally become larger. Even the conventional UK produced wagon and drags (right) have sprouted extra axles as an indication of how much heavier weights are now being carried. R830 HFT was given to driver Billy Cowell when new into service in late 1997. Built by Transporter Engineering of Gosfield in Essex, the outfit is based on a design of the old Hoyner concern. Modern day car carriers don't come cheap as this outfit reflects an investment of £120,000.

An articulated outfit hauling a drawbar semi-trailer (usually referred to as a double bottom) has never been generally allowed in the UK. There were trials of the concept during the mid 1970s as it was argued that the use of a larger roadtrain was quite safe on the motorway network and would cut down on the use of a smaller vehicles. The outfit pictured is using two identical Crane Fruehauf semi-trailers each of 23' overall length. Although the full outfit wasn't really practical to deliver round the back of the local high street, the rearmost trailer could be dropped off at a suitable point and shunted by another tractor unit. To head up the 38 tonne roadtrains, it's not surprising that the Volvo F88-290 was used. While the maximum weight in the UK at that time was only 32 tons, the F88s were rated as suitable for something like 52 tons gross operation because of the higher weights allowed in Sweden.

Below: Due to the framing of some long established legislation, a certain number of hauliers have gone back in time and in the 1990s were operating rather strange looking ballasted tractor and drawbar trailer combinations. What they've found by checking the law book is that it's always been possible to haul trailers up to 40 tons gross provided they're moved by a locomotive. Denby Transport of Lincoln is one haulier who's been operating three drawbar outfits at a gross train weight of 57 tonnes. The haulier used this method of operation as a way of moving semi-trailers which had legally operated on the Continent but once they left the UK docks, would have been overweight on a conventional artic. Although being heavier on fuel and limited to lower speed limits than normal HGVs, a small niche has been found for this form of specialised operation.

Above: WH Bowker had eight of these Volvo F10 Eurotrotters specially built for their Phillips contract to work out of Eindhoven in Holland. The Eurotrotter was a day cab'd vehicle fitted with a roof top sleeper pod although the Bowker spec' included lowering the engine to reduce the overall running height just under 4 metres (a standard pre-requisite for continental operation). These outfits - new in August 1989 - carried two interchangeable bodies - both 8.05 metres long. Although fleet no. 114 was sold in 1997, the similar 118 was still in use in '99 as a Preston shunter. Long serving Bowker man Brian Rollins was the regular driver of this European worked Volvo.

EIGHT WHEELERS

Although they're in use in all parts of the world, the rigid eight wheeler is something of a Classic British Animal. First conceived in 1930, they were long considered as many fleet's foremost flagship.

Changes in legislation, however, starting in 1964 were to leave the eight wheeler behind. Four axled artics were allowed to step up to 32 tons while five and six axled versions have been grossing 38 tonnes since the mid 1980s.

In 1999 artics could operate at 40/41 tonnes so there was a big payload deficit to the 32 tonne rigid eight. They may be classed now more as a specialist vehicle - suited perhaps for tipping work or when off road terrain is encountered - but they certainly had their day.

The reason for the eight wheeler's big attraction was a mixture of practicalities and economics. The early articulated outfits from the likes of Scammell had a mixed reception. Unlike today when the joy of articulation is being able to change semi-trailers so quickly, the early outfits were designed to operate as fixed outfits.

Not every driver liked vehicles that would bend (and jacknife) in adverse weather conditions while not everyone could reverse these cumbersome machines long before power steering became standard fitment. Early artics were also limited to 16mph while the eight wheeler could legally run at 20mph.

To the operator, the prospect of a (minimum) 15 ton payload from a 22 ton gross rigid eight was very attractive. A forward control cab (flat fronted) also allowed for the maximum amount of space although Joe Public was still bemused with those early eight wheelers: 'Do all those four front wheels turn at the same time when you turn the steering wheel,' was a regular query.

Shrewsbury based Sentinel was apparently the first UK manufacturer to take advantage of changes in the Road Traffic Act which allowed the creation of the rigid eight wheeler. In 1930 they unveiled their steam powered DG8 which sported solid tyres and chain drive. This Dudley & Blowers Green eight wheeler was an S8 - the more modern looking subsequent replacement - and it's pictured when new in November 1933. The vehicle was registered FD 8118. Although the law makers allowed steam powered eight wheelers to operate up to at 23 tons (diesel & petrol powered ones could only then gross 22 tons) as a concession to the weight of water and coal they had to carry, the subsequent 1933 Excise legislation was to prompt the steamer (and Sentinel's) demise. This stated that the road fund licence for a goods vehicle was calculated on its unladen weight. As the S8 was around a ton heavier than the first AEC eight wheelers, it proved a big financial penalty for any operator who continued to use them.

The Associated Equipment Co Ltd (AEC) are credited with being the first non steam powered manufacturer of the rigid eight with their Mammoth Major appearing in early 1934. In fairness this was a simply a rigid six wheeler with an extra axle spliced onto the chassis which didn't even have brakes fitted. Although it had an auxiliary two speed gearbox behind the main 'box, this really only created two top gears. The AEC diesel engine then fitted had a capacity of 8.8 litres. KCP Co. (Kirby's Country Produce) were to be big AEC users and this Mark I dates from 1934. Although doing haulage, they also did a lot of feed storage - and distribution round the local farms - at their depot in Little Glen near Blaby for producers like Silcock Feeds. Founder was Arnold Kirby and although KCP grew to a fleet of 20-30 it wasn't nationalised. Instead, there was a huge sale of the dark blue vehicles in 1948. The Kirby descendants did go on to establish the company of Federated Conveyors Ltd. The Hemphill AEC was a Mark II Mammoth Major from 1936. This tanker operator was later taken over by the P&O concern.

Established in 1829, JW Cook & Co Ltd were a large shipping concern based on Millwall Wharf in London. Diversifying into road haulage under the banner of Eastern Roadways, by the end of the late 1930s they had a long distance fleet of 250 vehicles. Mick Bradley joined the company straight from school at the age of 14 and learnt his engineering craft at ER's Bishops Stortford main depot & repair works where in 1949 was given the grand title of Group Maintenance Superintendent when the fleet was absorbed into BRS. Mick recalls that all the big operators made a move to the rigid eight but in 1934 all ER could buy was the AEC Mammoth Major Mk II. Four were bought (fleet no.'s 74-77) but their early 7.7 indirect injection engines proved rather unsatisfactory - at least when compared to Scammell six wheelers and artics fitted with early Gardner engines. In 1936, ER bought six Gardner 6LW powered ERF eight wheelers which proved pretty reliable - but not that quick. One noteworthy incident of fleet no. 78 occurred in 1947 when driver Cyril Whitmore overturned his vehicle at Littleport, Cambridgeshire. Cyril was unhurt while his ERF was righted - having lost its body carrying 200 sacks of malt - by a Meadows petrol engined ex WD Guy Otter gun tractor used by ER for recovery work. As soon as Scammell began building the rigid eight - 1937 - ER actually ordered eight vehicles but because of the war, they weren't delivered until 1947. Suffolk Road Transport was a subsidiary in the large ER group together with Days Transport of Ipswich, TC Grange of Wells, Norfolk and Orwell Transport of Ipswich.

Albion entered the eight wheeler market in January 1937 when they announced their T561 22 tons gross 8x4. This was offered with either an Albion 110bhp six cylinder petrol engine or the Gardner 6LW diesel. The model was short lived and by early '38 the CX7 took its place again with the option of the Albion petrol engine or a 9.084 litre Albion diesel (105bhp at 1,800rpm). The Stevinson Hardy CX7 EYL 519 was amongst the first built in '38 while the Arthur Wood tanker was built in 1945. The price of a new CX7 8x4 chassis in 1938 was £1,650 and with a dry weight of 5 tons 10cwt, a platform bodied vehicle could carry a clear 15 tons payload. When road tested by Commercial Motor, the CX7 (with the optional overspeed fifth gear) could do 32mph. Good performance of the brakes were remarked on although they were only vacuum assisted hydraulic on just six wheels. The hand brake got specific praise as it was also vacuum assisted.

25th September 1949 was a monumental day in the history of W H Bowker for on that day, all the 85 vehicles then in service were taken into Government ownership as part of the programme of nationalisation. These two photographs were taken at that time as part of the record of what the company were then operating. The Leyland Octopus BV 8074 was a TEW15T ch.no.15883 and new to Bowkers in January 1938. Strangely Bowkers themselves weren't taken over as they had the sense to set themselves up in the trade of storage and warehousing - which wasn't part of the compulsory purchase programme. William Henry Bowker started business in Craig Street, Blackburn during 1919. The company was incorporated in 1941 and at the time of the BRS take over, also had depots in Leeds, Liverpool and London. The old Bowker Stanfield Street base was to become the BRS Blackburn depot.

Bowker's storage business was based at Hollin Bridge Street and this was to be the company's transport depot when they started back in haulage during 1954. Like many at the time, the re-start was done through buying ex British Road Services vehicles (who in turn had bought these from private hauliers during nationalisation). CRJ 493 was an Octopus 220/1 chassis no.470074 and first owned by North Western Transport Services in June 1947. JTF 732 was ch.no.483118 and like the Octopus JTF 733 was new to R Rathbone in August 1948. Fleet number 17's load of apples & pears is a reminder that in their time, Bowkers were apparently the largest haulier out of London's Covent Garden market. The company also lays claim to being one of the pioneers of the night trunk system - with day shunters in the capital - when they ran from Liverpool to London during the National Strike of 1926. In 1999, the privately owned family concern (in the hands of the second generation) were operating 150 vehicles plus 350 trailers.

Unless you were involved in haulage during the late '40s and 1950s, it's difficult to understand how big an effect was the political creation of British Road Services. If it wasn't bad enough having your long distance general haulage vehicles compulsorily purchased, you then had to go into the lottery of buying ex British Road Services vehicles, primarily to get your hands on their important carriers licences. Bob Rankin (top) was a long established Leyland man but he was obliged to buy this 1951 registered Foden FG6/15 which started life with BRS at Bolton. Rankins are perhaps better known for their subsequent switch to tanker operation but their roots are firmly based in dry freight predominantly sourced from Quayside operations on the River Tyne. Daniel Smith of Larkhall had seen all his vehicles taken in May 1949 but five years later was to buy the 10 strong operation of BRS Wishaw when it came up for disposal. A strong Atkinson man, he too had no qualms about buying two Maudslay Meritor eight wheelers (TMG 700 dates from 1948 and started life in Middlesex while the second one was KXV 388).

In contrast to free enterprise hauliers, British Road Services could literally pick and choose which vehicle manufacturers they could buy from, such was the strength of their purchase power. Leyland and Foden eight wheelers were bought in large numbers but during 1952, the decision was made to have the company of Bristol manufacture both maximum weight articulated outfits and rigid eight wheelers. This was possible as the Bristol concern had also been taken into Government ownership in 1947. According to Allen Janes & Phil Sposito's excellent book 'Bristol Goods Vehicles', 105 AHW was chassis number 132044. New into service during October 1957, it was first allocated the fleet number of 5G328.

For some reason Albion were never prolific manufacturers of the eight wheeler but I've always felt their Caledonian was something special. It was only built during the period 1957 to 1960 and although it sported many Leyland parts - including the 9.8 litre Leyland 600 engine which produced 125bhp at 2,000rpm - many drivers reckoned it was a better handling machine than Leyland's well used Octopus. Three different Caledonians were produced they being the 24C/1; the 24C/3T which was intended for tipper operation and the 24C/5 which had a set back front axle. The first 24C/1 was noted for its lightness as the 6 tons 6cwt in chassis cab form equated to a 17 ton payload at 24 tons gross. Top speed through the five speed gearbox was 36mph while the first braking system (on only six wheels) was air assisted hydraulics. Although the Leyland Octopus - mouth organ front - cab was standard both these Shell Mex-BP tankers sport variations to the norm. UYP 839 dates from 1958 while the 24C/5 WUU 653 was new in 1959. Its 4,000 gallon capacity tank was built by Alfred Miles and the forward step cab by Duramin Engineering Co Ltd.

The Seddon eight wheeler was only produced in modest numbers from a start off date of 1958. 964 NUR was the pride and joy of driver Dick Bass who drove it from new in 1962, until 1968. Seen pumping out at Norwich Gas Works, Dick and the Seddon were actually based at Watford but collected liquid petroleum gas from Esso's Fawley plant near Southampton and delivered it across all parts of East Anglia. This procedure went on while the area was being converted from Town to North Sea gas. Dick recalls the strange characteristics of the product meant only 3,000 gallons of LPG were carried during the winter months although 3,500 gallons could be carried at the same 24 tons gross during the summer. The Seddon (named 'Spotty Maldoon') had the similar Gardner 6LW engine - David Brown transmission as Eastern's two other LPG tankers, the Dennis Jubilants 80 MAR and 162 NAR. Because the tank was made of 1" steel plate, unladen weight of the Seddon was 16 tons.

Of all the classic British built eight wheelers, the Mark 5 AEC Mammoth Major was a particular driver's favourite. Their smoothness and lightness of the steering, clutch and brakes meant that in the early '60s, they were an utter joy to drive. As a nationwide supplier of all grades of fuel oils, Stevinson Hardy's HQ was at Stevinson House in Fenchurch Street, London with depots also at Bromborough Port, Birmingham, Bristol and Barry Dock. Siddle Cook's HQ was at Transport House on Sherburn Terrace, Consett and although 6400 PT seems a fairly conventional eight wheeler, it was used for a variety of jobs by drivers like George Walker. Fitted with a 11.3 engine and six speed box (giving a 50mph top speed) it also had a drawbar hitch plus a turntable mounted in the body floor. Although a normal load of Consett steel may be on its back one day, hauling scraper boxes into Wimpey's at Southall for overhaul was also a regular job.

From the mid 1960s, the eight wheeled rigid always lagged behind the articulated outfit when maximum operating weights were considered. However, one area where the rigid usually outshone its flexible counterpart was off road work while Foden's distinctive half cab gave these vehicles a look and air of their own. Ted Ambrose of Chesterfield ran several of these Good Year tyred eight wheelers including URA 384F and URA 387F. The former was a 8L6/26 model having the Leyland 680 Power Plus engine and 15 cubic yard scow ended steel body. Rated for 30 tons gross operation (when off road) unladen weight was 10 tons 16cwt 78lbs. Ambrose also had a depot at Winsford and although the name is still in use, the company did sell out to Ruttles. The Tarmac half cab partially out of shot is believed to be BDA 706H.

DIAMOND T 980 / 981

There are certainly larger battle tank transporters than the Diamond T 980/981s but arguably there are none with more charisma and sheer bloody staying power. Almost 60 years since they were first conceived - and 55 years since they went out of production - there are still some of these 6x4s fit and capable of a hard day's work. What makes their story even more incredible is the company who built them - Diamond T - was at the time, probably one of the smallest truck manufacturers in the USA.

Although built in the States, the tractor's design was really instigated by the British Purchasing Commission who had set up an office in New York during 1941. On their long list of things to be procured for the World War II effort were tank transporters. True, Scammell were building their Pioneer derivatives but these 'Coffee Pot' 6x4s weren't really strong enough (or being built in sufficient numbers) thus the approach to several US truck builders.

How Diamond T got the contract isn't really known, but from 1941 to 1945, something like 6,550 tractors left their Chicago factory.

Although there were two different models built, there was very little difference between them. The 981 had a longer winch cable than the 980 (500' rather than 300'). Originally the winch controls were mounted centrally in the cab although these were soon relocated to the rear of the cab.

The main source of identification between the two was how the 981 had a cable guide assembly in the front bumper and an extra horizontal pulley to the left of the rear mounted cable rollers. These extras allowed the 981 to winch from the front as well as the rear. Because of this facility, the 981 was often referred to as a recovery tractor (and the 980 as the transporter tractor) although the former's front pull winching ability was really intended for self recovery.

In typical American form, the Diamond T was an assembled built vehicle using proprietary parts: Hercules engine, Lipe clutch, Fuller gearboxes, Spicer propshafts, Timken-Detroit axles. The biggest physical change to the Diamond T happened in 1943 when a three seat open cab was produced. Intended for the North African campaign, it arrived too late for operation in the desert and so ended up in Europe as a cold driving compartment even with its canvas roof and side screens.

It was to be after the '39-'45 conflict that the Diamond T really spread its wings. In Australia they were used to head up massive roadtrains while in the UK it was the heavy haulage scene that was enhanced by their efforts. Those efforts covered an extended period and it's only in recent years that the big Ts have dropped out of front line work and into the preservation field.

When the first Diamond Ts came into service, both the British and US military had seen nothing quite like it. Almost 60 years on, the combination of 980 6x4 unit and a Rogers built 45 ton capacity drawbar trailer still has a purposeful look to it. The drawbar trailer was built to carry the 40 ton Churchill tank although is seen with a crated load of parts. Most of the Diamond Ts heading for Europe were shipped in partially knocked down form. They were re-built by a number of companies including Lep Transport of Goole, the Michelin Tyre Company in Stoke and Alexanders of Edinburgh.

The quality of these reproductions may not be the best, but the incident it recalls is certainly memorable. Graham Booth traced these photographs which were taken by Harold Carpenter of Liverpool. Harold admitted to being the driver of this 981 in Holland during 1944. He recalled as there was a long queue to cross one of the two temporary bridges, he naturally used the one which was empty. As can be seen, this was built for lighter traffic only and couldn't take the 60 tons gross weight. Three other Diamond Ts were used to recover this outfit and apparently the only damage was to Harold's pride. The load is identified as a 'Kangeroo', which was an armed reconnaissance personnel vehicle - in essence a Sherman without its turret.

Seen during the 1950s on manoeuvres, this trio of 981s plus a 980 painted in Coronado Tan are from 19 Company which was later to become 414 Tank Transporter Squadron. 414 was to be based at Bulford although 19 coy had its base at Ranby camp near Retford. Loaded with Centurion tanks and hauling Dyson 32 wheel trailers, all up weight in this form is close to 96 tons. In standard ballasted form, the 980 tractor weighed off around 18 tons.

Tank men of old will take one look at this photograph and simply say the word 'Tortoise'. There were only a small number of these self propelled guns built and they were to come too late for active service in the war. Weighing something like 65-70 tons, the load required the support of specially built Crane 40 wheel trailers - and the efforts of two Diamond Ts. Operated as part of the British Liberation Army, apparently 336 Company supplied the first four drivers of this roadtrain.

As early as the late 1940s, the Diamond Ts were being sold off as military surplus in a variety of conditions. Many of these vehicles were as new and although many saw peace time service with other Armed Forces (including Holland, Belgium, France and even Germany) others were used for all manner of work. With the original six cylinder 14.6 litre Hercules DFXE engine producing between 185 and 201bhp at 1600rpm (depending on how it was calculated) it meant that this New York based six wheeled tipper of 1967 was as powerful as they came. T men of old will admire the upright exhaust stack. The standard system ran through the chassis and out through the rear cross member. In this form it was prone to leak so the upright conversion was regularly done.

The Diamond T wasn't the quickest vehicle on the road. Although it sported two gearboxes giving a permutation of 12 gears, in standard form overdrive top only produced a top speed of around 23mph. It was its strength which many specialised operators liked and many Ts ended up doing recovery work. Of all the different jobs the Diamond T ended up doing, the drilling rigs of Pigott Foundations were still fairly special. The Ormskirk based concern operated something like 20 Ts although strangely all the stretched 6x4s were painted in different colours - to distinguish them from each other. These piling rigs were operated well into the 1970s although its believed that one ex Piggot T is still being worked in Cyprus.

Pictured hauling the infamous 'Abortion' solid tyred Crane trailer, FYV 740 and FYV 741 (ch.no.9800147) were two Diamond Ts that never saw military service but instead went directly to Pickfords about 1943. Apparently two further 980s - GLU 654 (ch.no.9800670) and GLU 655 - were also taken direct although it wasn't until nationalisation, that Pickfords fleet was expanded with a further five Ts (two ex Road Engines & Kerr - EGG 159 and 160 - two ex John Young - EGG 570 and 999 - and one from a Leith operator). The original Hercules engine wasn't the most reliable of power packs. Having indirect injection it was bad to start in cold weather and also suffered from cracking between the cylinder heads. Those still in service with the British Army in the 1960s had usually been fitted with Rolls Royce C6NFL 12.17 litre engines to take the Hercules place.

HEAVY HAULAGE

Most things in life are relative. What may be considered a fairly routine load in the late 1990s was something special in the late 1920s. This tag axle six wheel converted Leyland SQ2 of Rotherham Transport dates from 1926 and it did regular double shifted runs between Sheffield and Birmingham. The pictured driver is the late Walter May - who was also to fight in both World Wars. Throughout his driving career, Walter said he only went to Court once and that was when he was fined five shillings (25p) at Burton-on-Trent for having no rear light. When asked if the defect was due to an electrical fault Walter said: 'No, it was because the candle blew out.'

When Edwin Elliott bought his first low loader (this ERF which was new in 1936) he felt he was really King of the Road. Based at Bishop Auckland in County Durham, Edwin and his elder brother Joe had joined their father William in the pipe laying business. Elliotts were amongst the early pioneers using mechanised trench diggers similar to the pictured Allen Parsons 12/18 model (it could dig a ditch between 12 and 18" in width). Manufactured by the Parsons Company of Newton, Iowa (who were bought out by the Koehring Company in 1929) they were made under licence by John Allen & Sons of Oxford from 1930. This machine sports a 1936 registration. Edwin was to make a bigger name for himself when he moved south to York and painted his distinctive fleet yellow.

Wynns weren't the only haulier to operate a Pacific and the 'Pride of York' was certainly special. It started life with Wilment Construction of London while Bonallacks of Wakefield were to make its distinctive cab. Ex driver's mate Tony Hawkridge recalls there was seating for eight in the massive crew cab. Ex driver Roy Atkinson says the left hand drive 6x6 was very noisy and terrible to stop. The rear brakes had no back plates so oil from the chain drive and gear sprockets could easily get onto the brake shoes. Braking was enhanced after the Elliott team replaced the original rear bogie with one from a petrol engined Antar. The problem then was the acute angle of the prop shaft so failure in that area was regular. Top speed was hard to gauge as Roy can't recall it ever having a speedometer. It was an out of control fuel oil tanker of Hipwood & Grundy that caused the accident on the A56 at Lymm although injuries weren't too serious. While the tanker driver lost the end from a finger, mate Pete Brigham badly gashed his head on the roof after leaping out of the offside seat. Driver Ken Pitts and the other mate John Sellers (who was asleep in the rear) were badly shaken but unhurt. When Edwin Elliott died in 1975, it's believed the Pacific was sold to do recovery work in Co. Durham.

SPT 600 was new on 12.8.55 and at that time, cabs didn't come much bigger than Scammell's hand built version on their 6x6 Constructor. The Rolls Royce C6NFL engine was also the biggest of its kind although 45 years on, 12.17 litres producing 185bhp seems rather modest. What made Cooky's big Scammell even more special occurred during January 1960 as it began service then as an artic weighing in unladen at 26.5 tons. With Walter Tomlinson as its regular driver, the Constructor did all manner of work although it got no rest when Hills of Botley bought it in 1968. Why it wasn't cut up for scrap no one knows but George Lammey of Northern Ireland saved it for preservation in '86 and 11 years later he was to sell it back to the Cook family. Siddle's nephew Donald Cook is now its proud owner although its current condition will give Donald plenty work. It may look bad but it can still start and is driveable. Anyone who's read 'Moving Mountains' will be aware of the reason why Donald photographed his eight year old son Andrew sitting on this particular mudwing after the Constructor had been returned to County Durham.

Siddle Cook ran all sorts of vehicles in his time although he never bought any Diamond Ts (even though as war surplus they were modestly priced). He was apparently concerned about them not conforming to various UK regulations although this didn't put off many other operators. Edward Beck's of Stockport are best known for their strong following of the Foden marque although the 1950 registered 981 PML 804 did stay for a brief time. Diamond drivers of old may recall these 6x4 tractors for their tremendous pulling power, dreadful steering lock and very small mirrors. The abuse of civvy street heavy hauliers also saw the half shafts shear fairly often.

Although originally conceived as a ballast box tractor, as the war progressed the artic form of the Diamond T did appear. It was found easier to manoeuvre and while carrying similar loads, the artic was nine tons lighter than the drawbar version. The Military reckoned it was limited in capacity (maximum payload 30 tons) although such an observation didn't prevent Crook & Willington Carriers from using them for heavier weights than this. The biggest asset of the Shelvoke & Drewry semi-trailers for drivers like Harry Maggs was how quickly it allowed them to load or unload crawler vehicles.

Wynns were big users of the Diamond T 6x4, PDW 321 being usually driven by the late Bob Thorpe when based at the Manchester depot. Hauling trailer 555, the outfit is seen in Liverpool docks, a regular haunt for the Wynns men of old. The port had the large floating crane 'Mammoth' so all manner of heavy electrical equipment was exported to the world via Merseyside. Ex Wynns driver Len Dobie recalled that when he drove the Diamond Ts in the Army, the heaviest loads he pulled were 45 ton Churchill tanks. When he had the 'T' PDW 927 at Wynns, 100 tons loads weren't unknown. In July 1999, fleet no. 266 (now with a

Nash & Morgan cab) was still in one piece and in a dry garage at Witney.

GUY INVINCIBLE

It must be a manufacturer's dream. How do you create something which as soon as it appears, it simply takes the breath away.

1990 was to be the year of the Magnum when Renault literally stole a march on their competitors but 32 years earlier it had been the prolific Wolverhampton bus manufacturer of Guy Motors who had literally stopped the industry in its tracks. Although production didn't get into its stride until 1959, the '58 Earl's Court Commercial Motor Show saw the hugely distinctive Guy Invincible unveiled to an awe struck public.

Actually this wasn't the first sighting of the vehicle which the trade press had enjoyed. Knowing that something special was due to leave the Guy factory for Earles Court, they arranged a friendly ambush of an Invincible tractor which had been painted up in Wynns' colours, to get an

earlier inspection and photo call.

What made the Guys stand out so much was the cab. In the days when the industry were hardly trying to wean themselves away from the traditional coach built versions, Robin Guy's design threw down the gauntlet to the rest of the trade. With a bottom half made of sheet metal and the top half constructed from polyster fibre glass, the method of build was fairly unique.

But what really set it off was its angular construction topped off with a full width sun visor which meant that some drivers soon nicknamed this range of Guy as an 'Andy Cap' - a famous flat cap wearing cartoon character who is still seen in a daily newspaper. Not that the vehicle had any other obvious resemblance to this northern wastrel for in calling the range 'Invincible', the sheer aura created by the name ideally

It may have been bannered as 'The Height of Perfection', but the first public showing of the Guy Goliath range apparently upset the authorities at the 1954 Earl's Court Show. They reckoned this double piggy back arrangement was too heavy for the surface so Guys were requested to take the thing down. The model name lasted only a short while longer because following protests from the German crane manufacturer of Borgward that they had used the Goliath name for their vehicles, Guy re-named their range Invincible.

complemented this classic of a heavyweight.

True Guy used the identical shape of cab on the 'Warrior' range but these were specifically a lightweight model both in production and intended market - although hardly any of their subsequent operators paid lip service to this description. But few users could dispute the King of the Heavyweight's claim made by Invincible even though this name was something of a second thought and were it not for the strangest of twists, it may never have seen the light of publicity.

Historically the town of Wolverhampton has always been a hot bed of engineering. Sunbeam was one of its first contributors to the automotive industry, the manufacturer being famous first for their cars and then, from 1931, for its distinctive trolley buses. Somewhat earlier, the works had for its manager one Sidney Guy who in 1914 had decided to take the plunge by leaving Sunbeam to set up as a lorry producer on his own accord.

At the outset his early models were lightweight 30cwt and 2 tonners but by the end of the 1920s the Guy range had diversified beyond recognition. Signifigantly bus production had started quite early in their life although Guy were to adopt the same chassis for either goods or passenger carrying vehicles. With such a philosophy, a heavyweight six wheeled double decker was to provide the basis of their first heavyweight, an 11 tonner announced in 1930.

Proudly called 'Goliath' the petrol engined vehicle wasn't a great success. Even when later fitted with the then new Gardner 6LW diesel engine, the Goliath didn't shake the transport world and after five years it was quietly discontinued. Not that Guy Motors were faltering as the '30s and '40s saw the number of company employees rise to the 1400 mark. Their products were a mix of lightweights, military requirements and of course buses, the large build numbers being aided by the installation of a moving track assembly line in 1939.

It gives some indication of Sidney Guy's rising fortunes how in 1948 he bought out his old employer, Sunbeam, whose checkered past had seen it bought by the Rootes Group in 1939 and then by Brockhouse in 1946.

One of the Sunbeam employees at that time who found himself with a new boss was Frank Boydon who recalls that even as late as 1952, Guy (and Sunbeam) were still heavily employed in military projects. Not so much in respect of vehicles but more a case of armament work in the guise of converting anti-aircraft guns for automatic use.

Frank became involved in an interesting project which saw Guys produce rifle butts in a revolutionary product known as polyster fibre glass - rather than conventional wood. The man made chemical product was hoped to be easier to

work than that traditionally used but it was its lightness and mouldable qualities that made it possible for adoption into the vehicle side of Guy's affairs. Initially this was simply for internal bonnet covers but by 1954, Boydon and his growing team of glass fibre moulders were gradually being shifted into cab modifications.

After an interval approaching 20 years, Guy had made the decision to go back into heavyweight vehicle production. They announced a range of vehicles which embraced 4x2 rigids and articulated tractor units, six wheeled rigids and the flagship eight wheelers which were then limited to 22tons gvw. This must have been a decision which was made with a great deal of trepidation as the heavyweight end of the market was close to being sewn up by the established leaders in the field of Foden, Leyland, AEC and Scammell. But the timing of 1954 coincided with the denationalisation of parts of British Road Services and coupled to a huge export demand created an inability of the market leaders to give any form of reasonable delivery time for brand new vehicles.

In fairness, the new Guy range was something of a half way house because by using Gardner engines, David Brown gearboxes and AEC chassis', the Wolverhampton manufacturer was making the step upwards in a transitional mode by using a large number of proprietary sourced products. Even the new range's standard cab was made by the Willenhall Motor & Radiator Co and was identical to the one then used by BMC (Austin/Morris Group). To differentiate their verison, Guy mixed some of their new chemicals to produce a front mounted radiator moulding which not only changed the look, but also acted as ducting for the heater and engine air intakes.

It's not surprising that when Guy announced this new range in mid 1954 they called it the 'Goliath' a name they had used for their first and only go at heavyweights in the early '30s. What did come as a surprise was the reaction the new model created in Germany. Not that there was a huge demand to buy it but simply a protest from the crane builder Borgward who claimed they had registered the name 'Goliath' for one of their heavy lifters and if Guy continued in its use then confusion would be created.

40 years on it seems hard to believe how anyone could get muddled up between a wagon made in Wolverhampton and a crane made in Germany. Guy of course claimed they had registered the name Goliath in the UK in 1930 but not wishing to be involved in a dispute which could stretch into litigation, they decided to change the new model's name.

Trawling back through the archives 'Invincible' was discovered, a model which also dated from the early '30s as a name that had been carried for a

McPhees of Newcastle were big users of the Guy range, JJR 583 being new into service in early 1956. McPhees specialised in an overnight service to Wolverhampton and were big carriers of Consett Iron Company's steel produce. The standard engine for this Invincible range was the 8.4 litre Gardner 6LW which only produced a modest 112bhp at 1,700rpm and 358 lb-ft of torque at 1,300rpm. The 6LW was never built for drag racing but operators simply loved the way the engine would last for years. Not really loved by drivers was this Willenhall built cab. One seasoned traveller described it as an awful rattletrap construction which shook itself to bits in quick time and was very difficult to repair.

Seen when fairly new in 1956, HCB 931 was WH Bowker's sole Guy Invincible artic then in service - although Invincible eight wheeled rigids were also in use. Chris Gardner's extensive research revealed this Guy's cab was built by Fowler of Leyland, a subsidiary of the Fishwick bus operation, who also had coachbuilding interests. Powered by the Gardner 6LW, 43 apparently only lasted nine months before being written off in an accident. It was replaced in fleet by a similar Invincible but fitted with a Boalloy cab. All Bowker's new Guys were supplied through TGB Motors of Clitheroe.

short time on a four wheel bus chassis. This title had been dropped in favour of the evergreen 'Arab' but as Invincible had the same strong ring to it that Goliath implied, Guy felt the change wouldn't have any detrimental effect. Perhaps the only effect it had was in the free publicity which the dispute had created but by early 1955, Goliath had gone and Invincible was the name for Guy's range of heavyweights.

As a new entry into the market place the '55 Invincible wasn't particularly startling. The lightest chassis / cab eight wheeler had an unladen weight of about 6.5 tons and with single drive bogie, the 18' 9.5" wheelbase general haulage model was intended for a 15 tons payload. It was abreast with the market leaders in offering full air brakes as standard (some were still offering vacuum assisted hydarulic brakes) although as the norm, the second steering axle wasn't fitted with brakes at all.

With direct top five speed gearbox and 6.25:1 rear axle ratio, the Invincible could do 32mph flat out. This was in the days when this class of vehicle was still limited to 20mph. Gradeability at full weight was limited to 1 in 6 so for steeper terrain, operators could have the lower ratios of 7.75 and 10.33:1 back axles - albeit with a drop in top speed.

It should be remembered that wagon & drags - a rigid hauling a drawbar trailer - could legally run up to 32 tons gross which equated to about 22 tons of payload for a driver and his trailer mate. Many Invincibles were pitched into this line of work but with only 112bhp from the 6LW engine, it equated to just over 3bhp per ton, a miserable statistic viewed 40 years on.

Guys were to offer the more powerful Meadows engine (also made in Wolverhampton) in the Invincible range for in 1955, changes in legislation allowed for heavier weights all round. Four wheeled rigids went up to 14 tons gross, six wheelers to 20 tons while four axled rigids and artics could run up to 24 tons gross. The wagon and drag gross weight remained at the old level of 32 tons gross, a figure it would hold until the early 1990s. Guys were in a good position to implement the modest uprating as when the Invincibles were announced the export eight wheelers were rated for 25 ton gross operation.

Exporting had always figured strongly in the Guy market place. The joy of receiving a repeat order for distant parts was an accolade that brought the response: 'That's another feather in our cap'. With so many repeat orders creating so many 'feathers', the commonplace remark became a company

Before building their own Invincible cab, Guy turned to Boalloy to produce this distinctive version. While the bottom half of the cab had panels riveted to a light alloy frame, the top half was built in plastics. The same style of cab was also used on the Guy Formidable range of 20 ton gross tractor units. The Miller & Gordon fleet from Liverpool were regular visitors to my home town of Consett, 544 ETF being seen outside the bus drivers canteen. It was new in early 1958.

motto with an Indian's head being used for the Guy trademark from 1934.

Shipping vehicles abroad in fully assembled form was always a bit awkward so in order to minimise damage - but also reduce shipping charges - Guy had adopted a technique with their smaller Vixens and Otters which involved splitting off the top part of the cab so that it could be stored seperately. Many manufacturers of the day were also supplying vehicles in a form known as chassis/scuttle. This saw the vehicle chassis produced with the floor pan of the cab and part of the front bulkhead in place, but nothing else. Customers bought in this form either as a way of cutting down on the normal excessive delivery time or just generally to have a cab built to their own design.

Robin Guy, who at the time was involved in the design and drawing office, looked at what was happening in practice with (or without) the cab and decided to blend the practicalities together to enhance the range. He was totally committed to the new found chemical polyster fibre glass, but while still developing their own plans in house, Guy turned to Boalloy to produce a cab which would update the range when compared to the rather staid Willenhall version.

The large twin wrap round windscreen Boally product was really quite stylish for the late 1950s although it was perhaps no coincidence that it shared a look to the newly launched ERF KV cab. It was built in two parts, the base section being constructed round a light alloy frame with panels riveted to it. A distinctive waist line was the join to a top section built in plastics, this lighter half ensuring a weight saving of 2cwt, when compared to the superseded Willenhall cab.

The Boalloy cab was also used on a 20 ton gross tractor unit which was given the model name of 'Formidable' but this, like the cab it wore, was short lived. August 15, 1958, was the day when Guy shook the transport world and announced what was known as the Invincible Mark II as a replacement to all the similar existing models.

Guy Motors had two main production lines at Wolverhampton. The small track, as it was called, constructed Warriors and Otters while the big track was responsible for building Invincibles and the Arab bus chassis'. Pictured in early 1960 bolting the cab down is Fred Chambers while Ken Smith is seen fitting a nearside hub. George Clark is holding the engine on the next vehicle in line while Ron Lucas is a distant figure further back fitting brakes.

Even in standard primer form, the bonneted version of the Guy Invincible looked something special. In total there were perhaps 15 of these 6x4 units built for South African Railways. The best known one on the UK scene was YDW 521, a cancelled export order which Wynns of Newport put into service during 1961. While the three seater cab certainly seems spacious, some heavy haulage men may look at the chassis of this six wheeler and wonder whether it was strong enough.

Counting that 1930s bus chassis, I suppose this really was the fourth version of Invincible but denoting it as the Mark II underlined the huge transformation. Based on a solid workhorse performance from their '54 range of Invincible, Guy had established a good niche for themselves in the market place and although parts were still being bought in, the Mark II denoted a confident step towards self build production.

Like all new releases, the unveiling at the 1958 Commercial Motor Show was the culmination of a controlled panic which had gripped the staff since the model was announced three months earlier. It is in this stage of pre-production where faults are ironed out but the period also seems to throw up difficulties which were never really contemplated.

Sidney Guy had retired in 1957 but was still on hand to witness the interest the new Invincible created. Four years earlier Guy had almost taken the same show by storm when they announced the Goliath model. It wasn't so much the individual

wagon, but simply the way in which it was displayed.

A Wolverhampton pyramid was created with an eight wheeler supporting a six wheeler which in turn had a four wheeler on its back. The triple decker was bannered as 'The Height of Perfection' with a long glass staircase affording a view to the highest parts. Sadly the show's authorities said that the weight imposed through the eight wheeler's tyres was greater than that preferred so the mountain had to be prematurely taken down.

No such problems when the Invincible Mark II was unveiled although it was to be the Guy people who were now concerned about the numbers who wanted to see or climb aboard their latest creation. Not only was the exterior design such a big eye catcher, the interior offered a standard of driver comfort far above anything else anyone had ever dreamed of. The pleasure of it all to the people from Guy was that both the design and the build of the new Invincible - and its cab - was all done in

To the many people who know him, Arthur Duckett is something of a character. His interests - past and present - are best described as diverse but back in the early 1960s he was operating a seven strong fleet of tippers from his base at Alstone Hall, Highbridge in Somerset. To me, 'Alstone Countess' was the pick of the bunch and although the Invincible received a mixed press by some drivers and operators, Arthur went on the record to say how pleased he was about it. Between March and June of 1961, the Gardner 150 powered Guy was worked 22 hours per day and covered close to 27,000 miles. Regular runs took the tipper over Porlock Hill (steepest gradient of 1 in 3) yet Arthur reported the fuel consumption as averaging 11.5mpg.

The multitude of choice in the Invincible range specification meant it was of practical use throughout the whole spectrum of haulage. True, as the premium Guy model then in production, it may seem strange that John Young opted for the big Guy in 1963 rather than perhaps a lighter weight Warrior. Strength - both on and off road - was where the Invincible had the edge and it also reflected a good image especially on longer distance service to the Continent. The Harper & Mylrea eight wheeler with tilt style of body dates from 1962.

Siddle Cook bought their Guys through TGB Motors of Clitheroe but because of Cooks heavy haulage background, it meant the well liked Guys were tested to the full. Charlie Burnell was given the first 6x4 Invincible - 400 EPT - which is seen with a Cook built extendible semi-trailer. Versatile enough to carry all manner of long lengths (up to about 60'), the steel pole was apparently 11" in diameter and it ran through a 12" tube mounted inside the rear tandem axle bogie. Both a locking pin and a purpose built flange were used to ensure the pole remained in the desired position.

When Bill Barrack first looked at the Guy Invincible he reckoned he'd never seen anything quite as futuristic. Invited by the Aberdeen Guy dealer to have a look round the Wolverhampton factory was to leave a big impression on JG (Sam) Barrack's son and the haulier put many into service. What impressed the Barracks even more was in Guy's having a far shorter delivery time than many other vehicle manufacturers of the '60s. Similar to all the Barrack vehicles of the era, the Invincibles received evocative names as a reminder of Barrack's heritage in steam engines (which also were named).

house at Wolverhampton.

Taken in context with the rest of the vehicle, it could be argued that the cab is the last thing you think about and perhaps the transmission or chassis build was far more important. Whilst taking this belief on board, Guy went one stage better for by using an established drive line, they felt what they offered in the cab would give them a big edge over the competition.

It may be difficult to grasp 40 years on the difference in driver comforts which this vehicle offered. In the 1950s if you had two windscreen wipers you were almost king of the road. Your windscreen washer was a squeezy bottle which you worked by leaning out of the window and stretching round to squeeze onto the windscreen. As for a heater, you just put your top coat on - that was the norm.

Optional extras to a vehicle specification might say include a passenger seat or even opening quarter lights to aid ventilation but the reason why the Invincible cab made such an impression was that all manner of extras came as standard.

Yes it was standard to have twin wipers, windscreen washers, heater/demister and flashing indicators. If you didn't believe that then how about an interior cab light which came on when the doors opened or how about a socket for an electric shaver and almost unbelieveably, a cigar lighter. True having a radio installed was still listed as an option but who would ever of thought of having a radio in a wagon - only the very high standard of cab insulation of the Guy made it possible.

These were the superficial goodies but things got better. Warning lights were built in covering every aspect of air tanks, water temperature & oil pressure while as the various levels adjusted

themselves to the correct reading, the warning lights were set up to dim - not actually go out.

Once in motion, the driver had a hydraulically operated throttle and clutch with hydraulic assistance also to the steering. Even the handbrake was power assisted and the prospect of an overdrive top six speed gearbox gave the potential of a high speed, smooth performance. Putting the icing on the cake was how the launch of the Invincible II coincided with the arrival of the 6LX-150 - the latest engine from Gardners of Patricroft - ecstasy indeed.

Describing the Invincible as all things to all men may be over the top but Guy weren't being modest for what they offered was virtually every option of engine/gearbox/axle which was available as part of the standard build. You could have Gardner, Meadows, Leyland or Rolls Royce engine, even the newly opened Cummins factory in Scotland would supply Guy who offered a chassis length which was cut to a customer's requirements.

Maximum weight ratings of 24 tons gross for the eight wheeler was standard as was 32 tons if you pulled a trailer. The heavy haulage men were catered for with six wheeled, double drive tractor units which were rated for 50 tons operation while what caught the eye of many was a long bonneted version of this type of heavy weight destined for Australia.

With such an all embracing package it was natural that orders for the new Guy came flooding in. Not only were these from long term Invincible users like Pointers of Norwich and Bulkwark Transport but other high profile names like Wynns and Tate & Lyle also bought, which augured well for its success.

By 1959 Invincible II production had shifted into top gear. Guy at the time had about 800 on the

Augustine Bell (known as Gus) set up in haulage at Carlton, near Stockton, in the late 1930s although it wasn't until he'd completed his war time service that he could concentrate on running the business. As the fine print on this photograph suggests, it was a trunk service to the Norwich area which prompted his business to expand. Gus Bell did operate some Guy Invincibles but this wasn't one of them. Although he was to later set up the company of Stockton Haulage, he sold out A Bell Ltd - as a going concern - to Spinks Interfreight of Darlington around 1962. BUP 858B is thus a Spinks vehicle and is seen leaving South Durham's Malleable steel works at Stockton.

payroll, their products coming off two seperate lines. The big track was for Invincible and Arab Mark IV double deckers while the little track produced Vixens, Otters and Warriors.

Physically the Warrior and Invincible looked identical, both sharing the same style of cab, but under the skin they were entirely different. While the single drive Invincible eight wheeled flat tipped the scales in chassis cab form around 6 tons 12cwt, the Warrior Light 8 was almost a ton lighter. The meaty 10.45 litres of Gardner 6LX compared to the AEC 7.7 litre engine offered for the Warrior although the latter's performance was enhanced by driving through an Eaton two speed axle.

But even with the Warrior there were ample options which could be specified in the standard build. In fact it used to be a Guy expression that they would build anything although customers were asked not to request a standard model because Guys just didn't know what 'standard' was.

Even when the likes of Ready Mixed Concrete ordered say a dozen six wheeled Invincible mixer chassis', they weren't built consecutively. Variety was certainly the spice of life for the Guy production workers as a mixer may follow a tractor unit, then a double decker chassis be followed by an eight wheeler.

While the fitters at Longbridge making Austin cars on a production line had something like a three minute work cycle, the fitters at Guy had a comparable four and a half hour cycle. Working at Guys conveyed a great deal of esprit de corps and although it felt very much like a family firm, everyone was kept busy.

Biggest area of expansion in house was obviously cab production where 90 men were to be employed. A streamlining of practices meant that the bottom half - which was first made up from 30 different pieces of metal - was eventually produced from five separate parts. A three inch flange was used to join up to the top part of the cab which had its own inbuilt stiffener. The moulding of the fibre glass allowed double sections so that heater piping and electrics would be catered for and Guy did intend that if the cab had to be removed for any reason, it was done from this central waist line.

With a cab so much ahead of its time, Guy employees like Frank Boydon were in great demand to lecture to all parts of the industry. He explained the Guy philosophy of believing that while the bottom half of the cab should be substantial enough to afford protection in the case of an accident, the top part merely had to protect the occupants from the elements.

It was while addressing the Plastics Institute at Harrogate that he coined the similarity between the cab and a hat & coat as all the driver really required was to be kept warm & dry. Perhaps this is putting their needs quite modestly but for those who were lucky enough to get one, they felt they were probably the luckiest drivers on the road.

Almost without exception most drivers of the new Invincibles waxed lyrical over them. Guy reckoned they would only have a two year 'honeymoon' before other manufacturers revamped their vehicles and produced something comparable so 1959 and '60 were days of sunshine

Those who have ever climbed into the cab of a Guy Invincible will know that a smooth form of entry is a practised art. The problem of too small a door was one of the first tasks of the Jaguar owners after they took over the Guy business in 1961. The modified version of the cab saw a step incorporated in front of the wheel and the door re-designed to cover the modification. Bill Pendlebury was on hand to record this Invincible of Allisons coming to grief in Kendal during February 1966.

As part of their diverse interests, Bristol Industries Ltd had a Guy franchise through their Rhodyate Garage at Cleeve in Somerset. Their haulage arm, Western Transport, operated a large number of Guy four wheelers but retired driver Ken Durston recalls that 748 EHT was their sole Invincible artic. New in March 1959 (it replaced an old Scammell artic which was bought from BRS in 1954) it's seen loaded with reels of paper from St Annes Board Mills in Bristol destined for Hamsworth in Middlesex. The pictured figure is Charlie Elson who at the time was a senior driver at Western as well as the Union shop steward.

and haymaking.

Not that everything with the vehicle was perfect as a wide variety of applications soon reported operational hiccups. Siddle C Cook of Consett had accumalated quite a few Guys buying their new ones through TGB Motors of Clitheroe. Cooks soon took umbridge with the hydraulic throttle as they reckoned any diesel leakage quickly rotted the system's rubber covers. Guy soon opted to fit a conventional mechanical system of rods to get round this problem.

Cooks were one of two northern operators to take one of the strongest Invincibles available, in the Consett case this being 2100 PT. This version had the Rolls Royce 212bhp C6NFL engine, which put into context was the same power pack used by Scammells to power their 100 ton 6x6 Constructor. Guy mated this engine to the ZF six speed gearbox and splitter which in essence gave the six wheeler an ability to almost climb house ends.

Down the road at Northallerton, Sunters big RR powered Guy was 863 BAJ, it first being given new to driver Philip Braithwaite. Recalled as something special, the Guy however did have a habit of lifting a front wheel when powering off under load. Naturally the chassis rebelled at such antics and cracked at both the front and behind the gearbox & engine mountings. In fairness to Guy they never envisaged such abuse although the heavy haulier's fitters reckoned the design of the rear bogie's suspension didn't allow for sufficient oscillation so the chassis had to flex.

Back at Wolverhampton, flexing chassis' of northern six wheelers were the least of Guy's worries as the honeymoon of the Invincible came to a premature end in September 1961. The problems had first become apparent to the staff when instead of leaving direct for delivery, new vehicles were being taken up to the field and held in stock. The next odd occurrence in the factory was when strange men appeared and all they seemed to do was tie small labels to the 6LX engines going down the production line which read, 'This engine is the property of L Gardner & Sons Ltd'.

It still came as a big surprise to learn that the receivers were being called in as the debts of Guys were announced as £1.2 million. Marketing difficulties both here and abroad was the official reasoning to the troubles but at least the Receiver kept things going.

By October 1961 new owners in the guise of Jaguar Cars had stepped in to take over the reins and although little on the surface appeared to alter, the new trading concern of Guy Motors (Europe) Ltd was now the official banner of operations.

In hindsight it may be fairly easy to pin point where Guy had gone wrong. In offering all things to all men, the only one they had done a dis-

service to was themselves. It needed someone like Jaguar to take a cold look at things and identify that rationalisation had to be the key to recovery.

Of all the models then being built, the Invincible was to suffer the most in the company shakedown. First to go was the treasured standard goodies of heater, flashing indicators and even the cherished electric shaver socket, which became listed as additional options.

The mechanical spec' also took a battering in that the Gardner 6LX - David Brown 657 gearbox became the only transmission available. Even the number of wheelbases to the entire Invincible range was limited to five as the emphasis appeared to pass to the lighter and cheaper Warrior which then offered all manner of transmission/wheelbase options.

What the rationalisation did mean to Guy was they they could reduce their prices dramatically and so go against the trend in the rest of the industry. Instead of paying £4,335 for an eight wheeled Invincible (cab & chassis) during 1962, the 1963 list price of the same vehicle was £4,130. The equivalent Warrior Light 8 was £700 cheaper.

It wasn't all doom & gloom for the Invincible as the new owners instigated a variation to the standard 'Andy Cap' cab. One criticism it had received from the oversize category of driver was that the doors were too small. Even with a decent range of grab handles plus a step ring on the front wheel, getting inside for some was rather difficult.

Both the Jaguar and Guy design teams were tasked with overcoming this problem and by '62 the Jaguar option of incorporating a small step ahead of the wheel was adopted into the cab build. The cab door was thus extended almost to ground level (to cover this step) which meant that for the first time, the use of fibre glass had been extended below the normal waist level. But again, this new cab was listed as a £60 additional option.

Another change which the new owners instigated was by changing the type of handbrake to a conventional multi-pull Neate type. It had long been accepted that the original swan shaped handle type was a fine piece of engineering in its own right. The power assistance generated by the first touch of the trigger set the brakes whilst a full stroke and a half on the lever was enough to physically lock the back brakes tight. In the event of low or no air pressure, the system could still be operated as a manual multi-pull handbrake.

The only trouble with this superb brake was its cost in that the factory pricing for this mechanism alone was £125. This is put into perspective when you learn that a chargehand working on the production line fitting the brakes was only earning £12 a week. Fitting a proprietary made Neate brake was a dramatic saving.

All these updates were incorporated into a

special Invincible 4x2 tractor unit designated as the Mark III. For its first six months it was only available to British Road Services but by '63 it became the standard top weight artic unit. A subtle change of this tractor was a reduction in the chassis frame depth from 12" to 9" - to make it comply with SMMT standards for fifth wheel coupling - while it was also plated for 32 tons gross train weight, for overseas applications only of course. In the UK rumours abounded that weights legislation was soon to be relaxed but fate was to ensure the Invincible played little part in future developments.

Even though the new owners had breathed fresh air into the Invincible, the wagon was starting to show its age. A Commercial Motor road test in May 1964 said the vehicle was noisy, the tops of the door shook a lot and the heater was inadequate. In its favour John F Moon said the clutch was light, the gearchange faultless, the extrenal sun visor still a huge boon and at £3,390, the 24 tons gross tractor unit was still a good investment but really the writing was on the wall.

In September 1964, Guy released details of a range which by 1967 had replaced the Invincible and was to stay in continual build until February 1979. The Big Jaguar range - or Big J as it was named - was to be the last truck to bear the Guy name although in its time, the new model had several different owners.

In 1966, Jaguar was taken over by the British Motor Corporation (BMC) who in turn merged with Leyland Motors in 1968. More than 16,000 Big Js were to be made and although it clearly beat the Invincible in numbers, to many it could never match the charisma of the model it replaced.

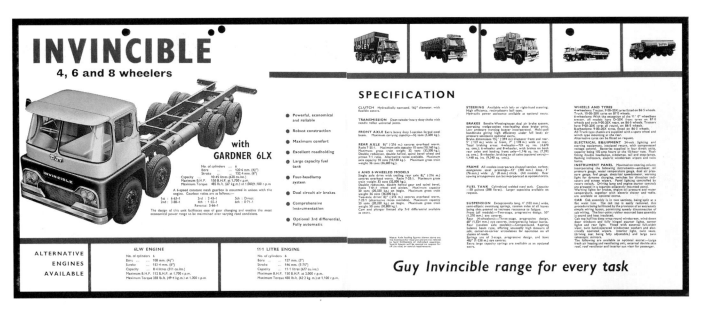

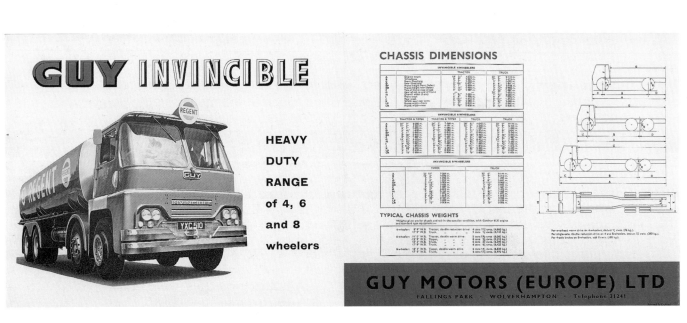

KINGS IN COLOUR

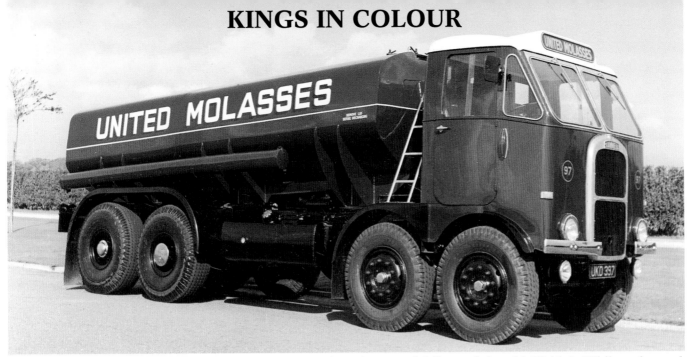

You don't have to be a Scammell devotee to appreciate the graceful lines of the old Rigid 8. While poise and elegance may not be words usually used in describing a vehicle like this, the United Molasses vehicle certainly has a very balanced look to it. While the company were strong buyers throughout the Rigid 8's 20 years of production, the drivers may have had different thoughts about them. Although these tankers roamed nationwide, the drivers were still expected to carry out their own repairs - as best they could. It wasn't unknown for some parts to be dropped off at a well known cafe (by another UM vehicle) and the recipient then fit them either on the car park or at any local transport garage who would let him use their facilities.

George Rotinoff used the Diamond T 980 as the inspiration for his Atlantic & Super Atlantic tractors, something both distinctive and special. Paul Hancox's research reveals that of the 35 Rotinoffs built, 11 are still in existence. This Roger Austin photograph shows Salvatore Bezzina's ex Swiss Army Super Atlantic near his premises of 1-3, Church Road, Marsa on Malta during June 1989. Chassis number 87001-032 was one of seven Supers and three Atlantics bought by the Swiss Army in 1958 (they later bought an 11th from the South African Defence Force). Powered by the C8-SFL Rolls Royce engine, this 6x4 tractor was sold to the dealer PLJ Europa in Holland on 10.4.75 who passed it to Jacksons of Misson near Bawtry. Mark Bamford was to buy the vehicle and paint it in the pictured British Racing Green (plus gold leaf coach lines) although it was later sold to Mark Walker who in turn re-exported it to Bezzinas in February 1985.

The S.34 was Foden's first tilt cab and was exhibited at Earls Court in 1962. The Robinson concern of Stockton-on-Tees were big Foden devotees but KUP 601C was to be a swan song. Not of the marque, but eight wheelers were soon to be phased out of the Robinson overnight trunk operation to Ware in Hertfordshire in favour of artics. Pictured loaded with steel vessels of chlorine, the eight wheeler had Tommy Simpson as its first driver. Because of his great expertise, Tommy drove many 'firsts' at Robinsons as he was the unofficial runner in of new motors. Strangely, Fred Robinson still spec'd the Gardner 6LW-120 engine (with 12 speed box) although this vehicle did more than one million miles without major problem. 'We only had one motor with the 6LX-150 engine,' recalled Fred, 'and three days before it was due to go onto the road, it was stolen out of the yard. Apparently it was later spotted doing local work in Abu Dhabi.'

The Twin Load was something special although Foden's alternative idea to the normal 32 ton gross artic never caught on. Fred Robinson said he didn't really want one although he was desperate to get anything: 'I went down to the factory,' he said, 'because they were late in delivering four artic units. Ted Johnson told me they would sell me any vehicle in the factory - and the Twin Load was the only thing suitable.' At the time, Foden were using the vehicle (on trade plates) to collect engines from Gardners at Patricroft. RUP 504D had the Foden Mark 6 Two stroke engine (4.8 litres producing 175bhp at 2,200rpm and 440lb ft of torque at 1400rpm) and would do a brisk 70mph - loaded. Used on the London trunk, Fred recalled the 16' 6" body on the eight wheeler was loaded for London, while the similar space on the Dyson built semi-trailer was loaded with smalls for their Ware depot. The day man would unhitch the trailer at Ware but as artics took over, the Dromedary was found to be too much of an oddity. After a few years, it was chopped into a 4x2 tractor unit although Fred still uses the old semi-trailer to exhibit a stationary engine.

OAJ 897M was given new to driver Mick Rowell and while seen with a Tautliner, was mainly used either on powder tanks or bulk tipping boxes loaded out of ICI Wilton. Although the 220 powered Borderers gave Prestons reasonable service, the problem they had was with OAJ 306M. This was the first Volvo F88-240 to come to Potto and the transformation in performance and ride quality meant that if drivers were given a choice between the new motors, then very few wanted to take an Atkinson. In their favour, the Atkys stayed around a lot longer than the F88s. Preston traffic office man Malcolm Hardcastle reported that the last of the old Borderers was used on shunting duties until it finally died in early '99 although long serving Mick Rowell is still going strong.

Wisbech Roadways has been a wholly owned subsidiary of Knowles Transport at Wimblington since 1958. The company never ran many Atkinson Borderers although Tony Knowles recalls that a good deal from Duffields of Norwich (then a Seddon Atkinson dealer) prompted his father Gerald to buy about six similar 32 tonners in 1975. All these were kitted out with an extra crash bar across the front grille, a Knowles trademark of the period. Why HER 806N sticks out from the others is in 1977 it was sold to Terry Godbold of Metfield in Norfolk. Terry recalls paying £8,000 for the Atky and its Seadyke tipping trailer. The deal proved a good one for Terry as the Atky (chassis no.FC29711) has stood the test of time. Its original Cummins 220 engine was replaced first by a 335bhp version (and later with a 350bhp unit) while Euro Axles of Stoke on Trent fitted an extra axle during its transition to a 38 tonner.

Dennis Smith recalls the five Volvo F88-290s he bought during 1976 were the first Continental manufactured trucks to come into his Bewick Transport business. Poor reliability of the then new Seddon Atkinson 400 range prompted the move although he later favoured Scania in preference to Volvo. The Bewick 88s were OEC 16 & 17P, REC 451 and 452R and TEC 571R. Pictured by Andrew Burton at Charnock Richards in February '86 (when John Watson was believed to be driving) 'Yankee Star' - all Bewick vehicles were named after famous American Pacer horses - actually started life in the colours of the Bewick subsidiary K Fell. It was usually first driven by Lenny Richards and it's recalled the vehicle only returned about 5-5.5mpg. Not as economical as the Gardner engines then in use, Lenny felt the 88 was out of this world when compared to his previous 'K' reg ERF. Apart from OEC 17P - which was written off after leaving the road at Sanquhar - all the Bewick 88s gave long service.

When new, REN 192S was part of the demonstration fleet of the Bolton based Mack Distributors (UK) Ltd. However, when William Dryborough approached the Mack dealer West of Scotland, they realised this was the vehicle for him: 'I want an idiot proof lorry,' he apparently said. 'Something very basic but which is solid and reliable.' Trading under the banner of 'Popeye of Scotland' the company operated a fleet of Scanias doing a lot of fruit traffic out of London. The dealer sold him this R685RT with the 237bhp Maxidyne engine and five speed gearbox. While none of the drivers seemed to like the Mack in the comfort stakes, it stood up very well to the six nights a week trunk service to London.

Jack Hill was a big fan of the Scammell marque in general so not surprisingly he operated a large variety of 4x2 and 6x4 Crusaders - including some left hookers - which were usually bought second hand. Not a lot of weight for XTP 324L, the sheer awkward size dictating the need for a police escort. The versatile frame trailer sports a steering rear axle and had three interchangeable girder frames. Originally built by Hands, it was modified by Hills to incorporate a hydraulic neck. This unintended stop in October 1977 occurred opposite the Studio B photographic shop in Tewkesbury High Street. Discussing the merits of awkward street furniture is driver's mate John Rawsley. The driver was John Millington who later left Hills to try his craft in Australia although he eventually returned to Botley.

It seems strange that while Pickfords took delivery of the only eight wheeled Samson - early in the life of the Crusader story - they didn't operate any conventional 6x4 tractor units until February / March 1978. Five 6x4 65 tonners then went into service with the consecutive chassis numbers 63004-8, registered UYL 809, 813, 814, 815 and 816S. While the fate of 816S isn't known, when 815S left Pickfords it got extended service with owner driver Brian Freer - a big Scammell fan in his own right. Brian recalls the startling performance from the unit's Detroit engine although with the penalty of a poor fuel consumption. Pickfords main concern when delivering this absorption column load was also engine related, but an extra spark arrester on the exhaust system ensured the delivery into the heart of a north west oil refinery soothed this concern.

Wynns 'Renown' was the only 240 ton crew cab Scammell Contractor worked in the UK in artic form. Based at Manchester, it was usually driven by Len Dobie although the pictured crew - with Len on holiday - are mate Ron Morris (left), steersman John Jarvis (right) and driver Brian Maloney or 'Bolton Bill' as he was nicknamed. The load is one of six 100 ton modules hauled between Pembroke Dock and Milford Haven during June 1980. Amongst the varied jobs of Len & Renown was the moving of around 300 straddle carriers (23' high, 14' wide) from Ferranti in Manchester to Salford docks for export. The first 14 mile trip took 11 hours but once all the overhead wires were re-routed, Len could do the run in 60 minutes. When this Scammell was converted to an artic, it was fitted with smaller tyres and higher speed diffs. Top speed leapt from 32 to 48mph although John Wynn's only complaint with this big versatile outfit was its road tax. In the days when artics were taxed on their unladen weight - of the whole outfit - it cost the haulier about £5,000 per year.

YGS 384S was the first Scammell Amazon 100 tonner to come into service at Wynns. Allocated to their Manchester depot, it was given to driver Brian Maloney in August 1978. Brian recalls it was actually taxed private for its first six months as Scammell had taken it to events like the Paris Motor Show to show off their latest Crusader variant. 627 is pictured carrying 50 tons of Turbine Rotor from Trafford Park to Peterhead power station during July 1980. The weight's being taken on a King semi-trailer which had railway lines fitted to its bed and a steerable rear bogie. Brian recalls the Amazon was slightly overated - when he compared it to Sunters Volvos and Scanias of the same era - although when operated in ballasted form, it still hauled up to 150 tons gross. Danny Kinlon was Brian's usual mate and his main complaint was the Amazon was about 12" higher than a Crusader: 'He couldn't leap back in when the vehicle was moving,' said Brian, 'I always had to stop to pick him up because of its height.'

RDC 318X was - and still is - a heavy haulage tractor of the highest repute. The French trailer manufacturer of Nicolas were keen to break into the truck market although they were to sell only a small number of their specially built Tractomas vehicles. The Sunter model was a TR66C4C being powered by an 18.9 litre Cummins 450bhp engine. Peter Sunter reckoned the vehicle did so well for them because it was allocated for only Albert Lowes to drive. In this Dennis Harris shot taken in March 1984, Albert is seen on Teesside with a 221' 2" long and 24' 8" wide, 303.4 tonnes column. John Woods is the pictured front bogie steersman while at the rear were trailer men Ivan Costick and John Garrett. On the nine minute climb up Billingham Bank, the two Sunter Titans were used to double head although Peter Sunter has seen Albert & the Tractomas move a load on site (totally unassisted) of over 1,000 tonnes. One thing Peter Sunter didn't like about the Tractomas was its thirst - it achieved only 1mpg when working hard. In July '99, dealer Mark Walker reported he'd just sold this unit for export to East Africa.

A444 PFC was new in 1984 to the Pig Improvement Company of Abingdon in Oxfordshire and spent its first five years - covering 500,000kms - hauling livestock to Spain and Italy. Bought by Laings of Hawick in 1989, it did a further 750,000kms in its next five years of service. The Cummins 290 engine drove through a Fuller nine speed gearbox while the drawbar hauling Ford returned around 7mpg. Although having a design weight of 44 tonnes, Laings operated the outfit at 32.52 tonnes which was ideal for its intended work. Hugh Laing reckoned the big Ford did so well because its regular driver, Jock Foster, treat it with so much respect. When Jock retired, the Ford was sold to Alan Pow of Bideford in Devon for preservation. Alan had previously restored another Transcontinental, the 4x2 tractor unit RLU 838R.

In the early '80s, Distington based Tyson Burridge bought two second hand Marathons from fellow Cumbrian haulier George Holliday of Penrith to work out of the Leyland Bus plant at Workington. Tyson's arm had to be twisted to make the deal because the preferred motors at the time were Gardner powered ERF, Atkinson or Foden. Surprisingly - to Tyson - the Cummins 290 powered 32 tons gross Marathons did very well. To denote the first presence of Leyland in the fleet, FAO 438V (normally driven by Ned Taylor) was named 'Tarnside Stranger'. Why the second one - EHH 478V - was named 'Tranter' isn't known - even by Tyson. Jackie Walters is thought to have driven this one and it's pictured by Andrew Burton at Crooklands. In contrast to his father, Andrew Burridge raved over the Marathons: 'It had a nice deep bunk,' he said, 'and its little steering wheel meant it drove just like a car. The gearing on it was just right and it would sit at 60mph no bother. The only problem I can recall was that they kept shearing front wheel studs.'

Sadly we don't see many Double Bottoms (or 'A' trains as they're sometimes called) in the UK and AFA 2316 is pictured in Zambia around 1984. Phillip Charalambous of Mufilira was one of Leyland Zambia's biggest customers so this Scammell built S26 was badged as a Leyland Roadtrain. With Cummins 350 engine and Fuller nine speed gearbox, the S26 was rated for 65 tonnes gross operation. In Zambia, this was translated to mean it could carry 65 tonnes of payload. Even overloaded, the S26 impressed its new owner. Bought to replace a bonneted Mercedes, the Scammell performed that well it apparently did one extra round trip a week when compared to its German predecessor.

Heavy haulage drivers who know the premises of Newall, Dumford & Jenkins at Misterton near Gainsborough in Lincolnshire will be aware that getting out requires a special manoeuvre - and ideally, an empty car park opposite the entrance. F16 driver Pete Elgie (with Wayne Upfold as his mate) has got out of more awkward places than this although the overalled figure of Jason Yates on walkabout is seen offering some assistance. There's only about 161 tonnes in this fertiliser dryer which was one of two photographed by Rod Spratley heading for export via Immingham docks. Heanor have used around 15 rows of modular trailer to ensure a lighter spread of the weight, the white coloured rows being of Scheuerle make and belonging to Team Heavy Lift of Holland.

If you have separate conversations with Heanor owner Peter Searson and Heanor driver Jason Yates, then you'll get two different impressions of the merits of H516 ARR. Jason will speak very highly of this 44.502 although Peter will probably say he'll never buy another MAN again because of this vehicle's thirst for fuel and poor dealer back up. Plated for 200 tonnes gross operation, the tractor started life in 1990 with Max Gohl in Germany. It came to Heanor just before Christmas '95 and is pictured by Kevin Cobb leaving Bridon Ropes at Doncaster with an all up weight close to 190 tonnes. Jason is driving while mate Darryl Hickingbotham is steering the other end of the outfit. It was to be problems with the ZF 16 speed gearbox & torque convertor which upset company owner Searson so the eight wheeler was sold and exported to Malaysia.

The Daf Space Cab wasn't built in as large numbers as the Volvo Globetrotter but it still had many fans. Penrith based Edmund Brewer has been sub contracting to Eddie Stobbart since 1982 and although he's built up a large operation, when he takes a vehicle out, he always opts to drive E680 XAO. He bought the 3600 ATi new in August 1987 and since then it's done some 1.8 million kilometres. Because it's regularly refurbished, it hardly looks its age but what Edmund really likes about the Daf is the way it has bags of character and is still a joy to drive.

Q753 BAU is quite rare as owner Chris Brailsford reckons the International 2275 is the only one in the UK. New in 1977 to the American Air Force, it saw service in the Middle East before being based at Alconbury. Prior to the USAF disposing of it in 1992, they reckoned it would never see road use again - because of its run down condition. They didn't anticipate Chris' desire to see it working because he found it ideal for Powerscreen haulage. With a 14 litre Cummins 350 engine and Eaton gearbox, the 6x4 unit is apparently very stable both on and off the surfaced highway. Pictured by Chris' son Sean at Barnsley, the load is an 85' long Mark III Powerscreen weighing approximately 15 tons. Although a head turner in this original condition, Chris transformed the 2275 by adding a high roof to it. The home made conversion utilised half the roof from a high top Ford Transit van.

Why should a modest Scammell Trunker be featured in a book entitled 'King of the Road' as in their time there was nothing at all special to them. The big difference to PVR 472J was it was very much out of time for even though it took to the road in 1970, it's seen during August 1996 still working hard. The reason for its extended operation was due to the desires of owner John Huddlestone and more importantly, driver Colin Rawson. Colin has a tremendous passion for older vehicles and while many people enjoy taking them round the vintage circuit, Colin believes you cannot beat simply using them for work. Powered by the Rolls Royce 220 engine, the Trunker was plated for 32 tonnes operation. It was only taken off the road in 1998 because of its heavy fuel consumption although it's not surprising to learn that Colin's replacement tractor unit was a 1958 Mark 1 Atkinson - yes 1958.

Also giving extended service was this Leyland badged eight wheeler belonging to the Stockton concern of Farrows. While their main business interest relates to cutting up metal, the Farrows enjoy both operating and showing their mature vehicles. This eight wheeler has been well modified in its 26 years of life although in '99 it wasn't in front line service. Instead Farrows were operating a TM Bedford which was a positive youngster as it dates from 1979.

What must be a contender for the swishest ever removals van (in Scotland at least) is M6 MSG, the pride and joy of the small family concern Grants of Buckie. When Murray Grant isn't moving the contents of someone's house around northern Scotland, then he'll be hauling freight anywhere in the UK or even onto the Continent. The FH12 Globetrotter is a regular award winner at most of the big Truck shows and in 1995 was an example of the best quality tractor then available. In contrast, the other part of the combination was a 15 year old, air sprung Continental built Latre step frame semi-trailer which the haulier reckoned was second to none for removals work. Bob Faulkner of Carnoustie was responsible for the Volvo's fantastic murals although like the Forth Bridge, Murray is continually adding to or even slightly changing the vehicle's appearance.

The FL10 Volvo is so much in use as a fleet motor, that they're hardly worth a second look. The one big difference to N917 WUJ is it has more axles than any other 'Wendy House' that you'd normally encounter. The specially built 10x4 is the King of the Sky Lift Nationwide Access fleet. Based at their Manchester depot, it had Stan Eccles as its regular driver. Although its number of wheels are of interest to a truck follower, its the potential of the hydraulic platform which is the biggest asset to Sky Lift. With an ability to reach 240' into the air, it gets to places that many other platforms cannot look at. One drawback to this FL10 is it tips the scales at 46.5 tonne and having automatic transmission, it's not the quickest motor on the block.

You're always going to be special if you're the first vehicle in a limited number of production. The first eight wheeled MAN heavy hauler with the V10 600bhp engine was this Belgium based example belonging to P Adams and the pride and joy of driver Edwin Lenges. Trading as Trans ADM of St Vith in Southern Belgium, the haulier is a regular visitor to the UK. Bill Kirsop photographed the new MAN in Europort coupled to a 3-bed-6 Faymonville semi-trailer. Although the crawler machine load from Belgium was destined for the Ipswich area, Bill said it was transhipped in the docks onto an HC Wilson low loader for the remainder of the journey.

Olympic was the name given to ERF's high top cab so it's not surprising that when Pollocks of Mussleburgh took delivery of P444 PSL in 1997 that it was named: 'Atlanta '96,' after the Olympic venue of the previous year. Scott Pollock recalls that they actually bought this ERF because driver Paul Cook was keen to try one. Its driveline sees a 380 Cummins engine power a 12 speed Twin Splitter gearbox. It's pictured by Geoff Milne at Washington Services on it's first Sunday run south and although Paul no longer drives the ERF, it's still used on UK long distance work.

The first Volvo FH12-420 Globetrotter eight wheeled heavy hauler into service in the UK appeared in October 1997 and went to Banks Brothers of West Cornforth in County Durham. It left the Volvo plant as a 6x4 unit rated for 150 tonnes gross operation while North East Truck & Van on Teesside added the extra air suspended axle. To ensure maximum productivity, Banks' crew the Volvo with two drivers - Ray Dwyer and Ian Harrison - although both felt their new motor would have to go some to replace their old 'J' reg F16-470 6x4. Although primarily used to carry Banks' own equipment round their open cast coal sites (which stretch from Northumberland to Derbyshire) the £225,000 worth of outfit is also used for third party work. Banks' bought the five axled Faymonville semi-trailer in August 1997 and at that time it was the first UK owned example of the Belgian made low loader. The Banks brothers, Harry, Joe and Graham, set up in business together during 1976.

Chris Bennett of Wilmslow is a long time fan of the Daf product but in search of more power he bought his first Volvo during 1998. The FH16-520 (plated for 150 tonnes gross) is a bit special in anyone's eyes and Chris reckons the big Volvo has proved to be an excellent performer. First driver was Peter Brookes and accompanied by mate Steve Blayney, they're pictured near Sheffield enroute to Immingham with this awkward - albeit light - vessel. Taking the weight is a Nooteboom semi-trailer with additional jeep dolly. Bennett's have preferred this option (rather than converting the tractor to an eight wheeler) and driver Brookes has proved himself very adept at being able to reverse such a cumbersome outfit.

The Eurostar was Iveco Ford's top of the range tractor unit when it first appeared in the mid 1990s. Hartlepool based John Codd's seven strong general haulage operation already had a pair of Eurotechs but John went for the bigger vehicle which offered a shade more power even though his 380bhp option is the smallest engine choice in the 'Star (there's also 420 and 520bhp options). Regular driver Tommy Rudd was said to be over the moon with his vehicle (and it's medium roof cab) which is seen hauling the lifeboat based at Filey in the 1960s. John Codd became involved in this fund raising project about 1995 which sees him taking the 'Robert & Dorothy Hardcastle' to around six shows a year. All up weight is around 25 tonnes.

The Space Cab Daf 95XF was to win over a lot of converts including Reid's Transport of Ayrshire. Company owner Robert Laidlaw was so impressed with the vehicle - and the Daf backup - that he dropped his total allegiance to Scania / Volvo and bought eight of these new XFs. Standardising on the 430 engine, the units usually haul bulk tippers however, this Bill Reid photograph shows one of the hauliers three Metalair powder tankers. There's no great significance in this Daf's name of 'Tillie the Toiler' as all the vehicles are named now. The big significance to this Daf's regular driver - George Tyson - is that he's been with Reid's for 27 years.

For sheer classic appearance, very few fleets can beat the Steven of Wick fleet. S171 JSK was given new to driver Gary Miller on 16th August 1998, it being their second 'S' reg Topline Scania 460 (Kevin McKenzie's S107 JSK was the first). The outfit is seen at Grimsby, a regular destination of the Steven fleet having hauled fish from the Scrabster market. Although Wick is still painted on the vehicles, the Steven operation is now based at Scrabster and the new dock area there. Gary says he's well pleased with his new Scania which is returning close to 9mpg. A personal Miller touch is the tartan curtains that were saved from an ex Sutherlands 3300 Daf heading for the scrap yard.

The MAN version of the Space Cab is called the Roadhaus. The cab was conceived in Holland after hauliers there began extending the standard cab upwards but rather strangely, Dutch MAN operators don't use the Roadhaus term - and look puzzled when you mention it. Their F2000s are usually referred to as Commanders or perhaps Benelux XTs. In Scotland, driver Vic Smith doesn't care what you call his latest motor, he just enjoys the extra space. Vic's 22.463 is Nicol's second Roadhaus (the 4x2 R89 KSA was their first) and is pictured with a Nu-Clean, Valley vacuum tank. Nu Clean is a subsidiary of Nicols and involves the bulk haulage of material like drilling mud. New on 10.3.99, T860 ASO is only the second 6x2 unit at Nicols. The first was a 6x2 Roadtrain, C498 RSS which was new on 20.11.85. The late Willie Nicol apparently didn't take to the Roadtrain so it only stayed 18 months. Bruce Nicol reckons this MAN should stay a lot longer.

MACK – THE BULLDOG SPIRIT

Mack has never had a strong presence on the UK highways but the American truck builder (with its HQ in Allentown, Pennsylvania) has always had a close affinity with many British people.

Apparently it was the British Tommies fighting in World War I who were to create the link between Mack and the famous Bulldog mascot. So strong and gritty was the capability of the AC Series Macks at work in the muddy fields of France that the Tommies likened them to a Bulldog: 'Once the Mack gets its teeth stuck into doing something,' they said, 'then it never gives up.'

The gist of this glowing observation eventually made its way back to the USA although it wasn't until around 1932 that the Bulldog motif was first used by Mack. More than 60 years on this marketing symbol is still strongly utilised while the company even has a series of Bulldog lapel badges depicting the various roles Mack trucks are involved in.

Although it's now a totally owned subsidiary of the French manufacturer Renault, the Mack reputation of strength is still second to none: 'Built like a Mack truck,' is an expression which all Americans appear to relate to.

What makes the Mack so special in the UK is its rarity. Although they've had an importing presence here since the 1940s (smaller ones were even built here in the '60s) the numbers about are fairly modest.

Western Truck Ltd of Leyland in Lancashire was set up by directors Rick Roberton and Tony Bobola in the early '80s and they currently look after Mack's interests both in the UK plus other specific markets when requested to do so by Mack.

As part of the Richards & Wallington Group of Companies, R K Crisp Ltd had its head office in Tyseley, Birmingham plus a depot in Portswood Road, Southampton. Amongst their diverse heavy haulage fleet it's not surprising that HOM 201D was their biggest head turner. Identified as an RD700SX, the 6x4 unit was probably capable of moving anything up to 100 tons in weight. Like every other Mack produced, the vehicle came off the production line as a purpose built vehicle made to a customer's specific order. The distinctive cast spoke front wheels weren't that well liked by British wagon drivers but those in the know reckoned it was just because they weren't used to dealing with them. A lot easier to handle, they'd tell you, but don't overtighten the nuts.

P & S CONTRACTS

Mention the words 'King of the Road' to certain older drivers and they'll probably retort with the name P&S Contracts. Why George Patterson wanted to write that expression across the front of his vehicles isn't known but it certainly got them noticed. It also helped that his 15 strong fleet was made up of bright mustard yellow Macks - which seemed to go faster than anything else on the road while carrying a lot more weight. Apparently even the fish wagons of Charlie Alexanders used to pull into the side if they saw the five orange marker lights on the roof top of a P&S Mack in their mirror - they knew the Big Yellow Peril would soon be coming past.

Patterson and Small went into haulage at Baillieston, in the eastern outskirts of Glasgow, during the post de-nationalisation boom of private hauliers in the mid 1950s. When his partner decided to emigrate to South Africa, George kept the P&S name although it was very much a Patterson family business with both his parents also helping out.

George originally ran a fleet of Atkinsons (four eight wheelers and eight artics) but when visiting relatives in Canada in the early '60s, he saw how well the Mack performed so he decided to totally change the fleet. In 1964, the law makers had just increased the maximum weight for artics from 24 to 32 tons. However, rumours abounded that weights would increase to 38 tons, provided your artic unit was a double drive six wheeler.

This suggestion made George's mind up and within three years he'd bought three batches of brand new right hand drive six wheelers plus two left hookers which had started life in the Middle East. The first imports were BVA 637, 638, 639 and 640B; the next batch was DVA 79, 80, 81, 82 and 83C; while the last batch were GVD 636, 637, 638 and 639D. The 'B' and 'C' regs were B61s whilst the last batch were the newly introduced R600s. The two left hooker B61s (one was registered AUE 749B) were bought from a dealer in Warwickshire together with masses of spares after they'd been imported (second hand).

Importing new vehicles was made difficult for P&S. Something like £800 per vehicle was added on as an import tax and after being coupled to a 30' long Northern tandem axled semi-trailer, each outfit apparently cost £10,500 - well in excess of any comparable UK artic then on the road. In fairness there was nothing to compare with these Macks and while George did hope to become the UK agent for Macks, he first put their reputation of strength to the haulage test.

The main work for P&S was out of William Beardmore's Parkhead Forge at Baillieston. To provide an overnight service to all parts of England, P&S ran night trunkers to both Kelly's Cafe at Boroughbridge on the A1 in North Yorkshire (for east coast traffic) or the White Horse Cafe on the A6 at Coppul in Lancashire for loads going to the west side of England. Eddie Shaw was one of the shunters living at Boroughbridge while Mick Brady and Graham Ward were two of the P&S team based in Lancashire.

Jimmy Sloan and Alec Miller were two of the Baillieston drivers as was John Blythe who at the age of 24, didn't know what he'd let himself in for when first given the keys of BVA 640B.

What John got was a top speed of 62mph and an ability to cross the likes of Brough, Shap and Beattock in all weathers - because of the 6x4 set up - while carrying a bit more weight than usual. Even though the 38 ton rumours never materialised (in the '60s at least) John said that George opted to run slightly heavier: 'It was difficult to gauge the weight of some of the castings we carried so we probably ran closer to 38 tons than 32, but the Macks were more than strong enough for the job. The only thing which could travel as fast was the AEC Mandators but at the first sign of a hill, we'd leave them trailing behind. You've got to remember these were the days when the Gardner 150 was thought to be a big engine - in comparison the Macks were just terrific.'

P&S had another office at Rotherham above a cake shop as a lot of their traffic was delivered to engineering firms in South Yorkshire. The big bonneted Macks didn't handle very well in the confines of some of these works and Mick Brady recalls it wasn't unknown for him to ask an overhead crane driver to lift his trailer round a tight corner.

When the A1 in North Yorkshire was being upgraded there were a number of tight turns and one of the P&S Macks came to grief near Dishforth. A 20 ton mobile crane was sent to lift the stricken outfit but even after the tractor was unhooked, the crane driver was surprised that his crane just couldn't budge the loaded trailer.

The reputation of P&S was well known although the drivers seemed to lap it up - and try and live up to it. Having 195bhp from those first 11.59 litre Thermodyne engines produced the speed but to get it onto the road, the drivers had to master the 10 speed gearbox which needed both hands to operate the two stick shift.

When you knew how to handle them, the Macks couldn't be beaten although when running in tandem, it wasn't unknown for the lighter loaded outfit to push the heavier one up any major incline. Woodhead Pass over the Pennines was known for the hairy activities of the likes of Peter Slater's coal carrying eight wheelers but even they didn't dice with the mad yellow Scotsmen.

With such a reputation, it wasn't unknown for the P&S Macks to encounter the occasional challenge and Dennis Smith reckoned the motor he was mating always came off best. Dennis crewed the Leyland Octopus eight wheeler and drag with 210bhp Power Plus 680 engine (and overdrive top gearbox plus high speed 4.82:1 diffs) which Eric Postlethwaite drove for Bradys of Barrow-in-Furness. 'With a top speed of 92mph,' he reckoned, 'the Octopus could leave those noisy Macks no bother especially up Beattock and especially fully freighted. And when I say full, we always ran full.'

The shunters had to pedal harder than the trunk drivers while the most difficult job for the Coppul team was if their load was destined for the Steel Company of Wales in Newport. The trunker normally got to the White House at 12 midnight but it meant there was no rest if the shunter had to get down to Newport then tip and load again to be back in Lancashire for the following midnight. Yes, drivers hours rules were also stretched at times.

While P&S gave their customers a good service, one thing they couldn't prevent was the railway linked Freightliner business being able to undercut their rates. After P&S went into liquidation during 1969, George Patterson decided to emigrate to Canada. He tried to re-export his four latest R600 tractor units to operate over there (he even asked Eddie Shaw if wanted to emigrate with him) but apparently this move was blocked by Government red tape. Instead, they were sold to HG Pentus Brown of Leighton Buzzard and used to haul powder tankers. Strangely, not many others expressed interest in buying the old B61s.

In their short time, P&S made a big impact although the experience did John Blythe a lot of good. He went on to be an owner driver for 15 years but coming to terms with a mundane Atkinson Borderer was almost an unreal experience after his five years behind the wheel of a big yellow Mack.

Once seen, never forgotten thought Tom Riding when he photographed the P&S Macks at the White Horse Cafe at Coppul in February 1966 (left and previous page). Tom may have been used to seeing rather normal vehicles in the family's W&J Riding fleet but at the time, the P&S fleet was considered by many wagon drivers as the real King of the Road. P&S owner George Patterson also ran a Rolls Royce car but the strength of that fine British machine was put to the test after he tried to tow start one of his Macks in Rotherham. The Roller came off second best as the Mack wouldn't move and George simply tore off his bumper.

Not many Mack DM (dumper/mixer) chassis' were sold in the UK but the Darlington based civil engineering concern of William Press were to buy two of them about 1977. They also bought this Crane four axle girder trailer but although the Macks were new, the load carrier started life with Elliotts of York. Sadly the pull push outfit didn't see service in the UK as it was bought specifically to work at Togo, in East Africa. At that time, Press' were building an oil refinery and the girder outfit was used to carry large vessels from the nearest port to site. The William Press business was founded in the early 1900s although the family name was actually Allpress. After merging with the Fairclough and Mathew Hall business', the late 1980s saw the dropping of the Press name in favour of the AMEC title.

Ian and Hardy Brown bought this F786T in October 1976 to use in their contracting business in Perth although as the TIR badge indicates, the company also ran fridge vans on Continental work to Holland, Belgium and France. Browns bought three Macks through the Scottish dealer West of Scotland Excavations Ltd the second one being the similar OES 30R. This latter vehicle had Alex Steel as its regular driver who soon became a big fan of the Mack's huge bunk - and its brisk performance. Apparently comparing the Mack to Alex's previous unit - an MAN - saw the Bulldog save two hours on the journey time between Perth and the coastal ports in southern England. While the standard performance of the 11.82 litre 306bhp Mack engine was good, you should ask the Browns about the tinkering they did on 'The Pig', and honestly, just how fast would that go.

RJ (Bob) Norman of West Road, Pogmoor, Barnsley was to operate about six Mack R685RT tractor units although 'Midnight Star' was their first. With a design weight of 38 tonnes, the vehicles were used for the bulk haulage of scrap, coal and aggregates. As its name suggests, the Neville Ratesaver semi-trailer was lighter than some as the tipping body also doubled as the trailer chassis. The tractor units were also fairly light as Bob Norman quoted them as being under 5.5 tons and averaging between 7.5 and 8mpg - when working hard. Geoff Milne's protracted research reveals other Norman Macks bought new as: 'Glory' SKY 611S; 'Hobo' SKY 612S; 'Zulu' YWE 784T; 'Demon' YWE 785T; 'Fury' RWE 449X and 'Revenge' XEN 161T. All the individual names were prefixed 'Midnight'.

Garston Port Services was a long established Merseyside ship's chandler concern owned by the Darnell family who also operated a fleet of 10 vehicles in the late '70s. While Tommy Shire drove this F786T, Ron Cheetham had the second Mack on fleet YVM 312T. Regular work for these two left hookers was to carry central heating radiators from KME in Kirby across to Ireland. Beef was then loaded into the refrigerated trailers for delivery to the American military bases in Germany. Ron recalls the three, trouble free years on his Mack with great enthusiasm. He said the performance of the 306bhp Maxidyne engine with seven speed Maxitorque gearbox was phenomenal. This was borne out when Truck magazine road tested Tommy's wagon in April '78. On the two day test run, fuel consumption was also a credible 7.16mpg when running at 32 tons gross. Price of the new Mack at that time was given as £23,833. Other new vehicle list prices at the time were £20,810 for the revamped Leyland Marathon 2 and £22,250 for a just announced Volvo F10.

UDT 61S was an F786ST operated by McErlain Plant Ltd, a subsidiary of the various operations belonging to Patrick McErlain. Plated for 110 tonnes gross operation, the 6x4 tractor had the 306bhp Maxidyne engine and 12 speed Maxitorque transmission. Used mainly to carry the company's own plant and equipment, it did haul machines to McErlain's own site in Belgium. Seen on its first trip to collect a Poclain 300CK from Hook in Hampshire (grossing around 85 tonnes) the pictured driver is Dave Hill. Dave didn't stay with the Mack too long as Peter King drove it most - a low loader driver of the highest quality, said David McErlain. After the company was taken over by Northern Strip Mining, the Mack passed to Hills of Blackwell. It subsequently ended up with a Circus owner and the last time it came into Chesterfield, it was hauling a load of elephants.

West of Scotland Excavations Ltd was established in the 1940s when James Campbell went into plant hire and the earth moving business. His first Mack was actually an ex war time petrol powered one although in the mid '70s the company was to buy nine new ones as they became the Scottish dealer of the marque. XSU 410S was the company's first 6x4 unit although for weights up to 50 tonnes, the company operated YGE 393S. Pictured by Dave Lee at Southampton docks, the Crane Fruehauf semi-trailer is supporting a 20 tonne Caterpillar 977 made in Scotland and going for export. The F786T unit was the pride and joy of the late Charlie Conwell. The company named their vehicles after Country & Western Songs and fans will know 'Phantom 309' as the song in which a driver is killed - saving a bus load of kids from an accident - but then comes back with his truck as a friendly ghost.

With a 150 tonnes gross rating, SGA 638W was West of Scotland's strongest Mack. It's pictured on its first job coupled to a WNC tri-axle semi-trailer moving a 24' wide section of a Marion face shovel from an open cast coal site near Shotts to the Wimpey depot at Uphall. The road haul was about 25 miles and all up weight was around 135 tonnes. Driver was Rob Menzies while his mate on this job was Sammy Grant. The FM786ST had a raised roof to incorporate a second bunk while the 306bhp engine drove through a 12 speed gearbox. The Mack only did this job after another unit broke down and only later received its individual name of 'Me and Earl'. West of Scotland came out of haulage in 1993 although Rob Menzies took up owner driving and in 1999 was running a Daf XF95.

Chris Brailsford said he was heart broken when he sold his Mack Ultraliner for customising in 1999. He'd bought the vehicle in '96 although it had started life with KTS of Rotherham in 1990. Rated as an 80 tonner, the vehicle had the 350 Maxidyne engine and 10 speed Maxitorque gearbox. Chris' son Roger took this photograph as it was enroute from Spennymoor to Burton-on-Trent with a 40 tonnes cement silo section which had a running height of 16'. Chris is a dedicated Mack nut so not surprisingly reckoned his old vehicle was perfect for this line of heavy haulage work. Fuel consumption wasn't brilliant at the 6-6.5mpg mark although it hardly varied no matter what the load.

SOMETHING SPECIAL

Not really a wagon and really, a strange looking drag. The perk of writing and publishing your own books is that you can always find an excuse to include something special like this. The Scania-Vabis 20 seater bus dates from 1922. The merged Swedish concern evolved in 1911 although Scania - based in Malmo - dealt with commercial vehicle production while Vabis, from Sodertaljie, built cars and dealt with all the group's engineering requirements. The Vabis part of the company title was only dropped in 1969 when Scania and Saab joined forces.

If the driver of this Australian based RFW insisted that he was King of the Road then I can imagine that few other drivers would wish to argue with him bearing in mind the cargo he was carrying. This explosives hauling 8x8 has a 475bhp Detroit engine driving through an Allison automatic gearbox. It's believed to have been operated by ICI Australia. RFW - Robert Frederick Whitehead - set up his specialist truck building concern at Chester Hill in New South Wales during 1969.

LENGTH—75'
WIDTH—11'0"
WEIGHT—9½ons
KEAY
DARLASTON

 Had not this photograph been taken, I doubt if anyone would have believed Dennis Hines when he tried to explain what his Birmingham based Bedford artic could actually carry. Although he has to be admired for even attempting such a move, the photograph just beggars belief. Calculations to locate the centre of gravity were apparently not a priority although it's not surprising when the load reversed out of the fabrication shop, the first thing it did was to partially demolish the wall opposite.

Scammell Rigids 8s were a regular sight although the Watford manufacturer only built seven of these distinctive 8x6 gritters for the Ministry of Transport during 1959/60. Roger Kenny had the foresight to record such a vehicle which was really an amalgam of four different Leyland Group vehicles. This distinctive snub nose bonnet (from a Scammell Highwayman) concealed a Leyland 680 engine while the second steer axle (undriven) was from a Leyland Octopus. The rear double drive bogie was from a Scammell Constructor while the two speed transfer box (which took the drive to the front axle) came from the Scammell Super Constructor range. Atkinsons of Clitheroe manufactured the spreader body while the vehicle also pushed 5cwt of snow plough when it was attached to the front.

As mentioned in the colour section, the Swiss Army was to be a very good customer for George Rotinoff. His first sale to them - chassis no 20 - is pictured hauling a Scheuerle trailer loaded with a Centurion battle tank. In profile form, the Atlantic is identified from the bigger Super version as the front overhang - beyond the mudwings - is 10" shorter. The Super also had two exhaust pipes that were a lot closer to the cab than the single stack of the Atlantic. In July '99, this Rotinoff was owned by Oakwood Plant in London.

The Rotinoff Viscount was a smaller and lighter version of the Atlantic. Built in fairly conventional form, it was intended for haulage work - albeit at heavy weights - rather than as a ballasted tractor. Only two Viscounts were made and these were operated as Roadtrains in Australia and both have survived - one at Alice Springs, the other at Perth. The rear axles in the Viscount were made by Kirkstall while the same type were fitted to the 40 ton Coles Illustrious mobile crane. The Viscount is pictured undergoing Army evaluation trails hauling a Crane 24 wheeler loaded with a variant of the Churchill tank.

The Rotinoff made its mark at Bradwell Power Station in 1957 and even now the feat of moving those 12 Head Wrightson boilers - 238 tons a time - from a 1 in 10 start, takes some believing. Sunters Atlantic gave about 20 years good service and being the first vehicle ever to move over 200 tons, it gave Peter Sunter a lot of pleasure that he could donate this superb vehicle to the National Science Museum at Swindon. Before leaving Northallerton in 1980, the Rotinoff spent 11 months at High Etherley where Ted Hannon restored it to as new condition. It was fitting that when the handover took place, Peter was accompanied by John Robinson (seen behind the wheel and on the running board). John began driving for Sunters (illegally) at the age of 16 when they were based at Gunnerside in the Yorkshire Dales and spent his entire 50 years of working life with the firm. Virtually every big heavy haulage tractor was given first to John while Peter sums him up by saying: 'John Robinson was simply Mr Sunter Brothers Heavy Haulage.'

Even in the late 1990s, the sight of this one off BP Autotanker would still turn the head. In September 1960, people just didn't have a clue what it was. The 4,000 capacity tanker was built by Thompson Brothers of Bilston and was destined to be used by BP in Denmark. The all integral construction saw the engine and transmission mounted transversely at the rear of the vehicle which was similar to the idea behind Leyland's then new Atlantean double deck bus chassis. Entry to the cab was via the single shallow door in the centre of the front bulkhead below the windscreen. It should also be noted that driver & passenger seats had full seat belts fitted.

BP 'AUTOTANKER'

KEY

(1) Rear-view 'periscope' lens. (2) Rear end hinges up for engine access. (3) Six-cylinder Leyland 'Power-Plus' diesel engine, developing 200 b.h.p. (4) Fireproof bulkhead. (5) Side radiator, with fan-assisted cooling. (6) Leyland four-speed Pneumo-Cyclic gearbox and clutch unit gives two-pedal control. (7) Internal rear bumper protects engine unit. (8) Angled drive-shaft to Eaton two-speed driving-axle, which in effect gives eight forward speeds. (9) Aluminium alloy integral tanks, with six compartments for varied fluid loads; welded by the Argonarc process. (10) Rear road-springs of Leyland 'Dromedary' chassis. (11) Top-loading hatches. (12) Periscope tube inside walkway. (13) Walkway along top of tanker. (14) Glass-fibre moulded external panelling. (15) Combined tank for fuel and hydraulic fluid (for pumping system). (16) Avery Hardoll bottom-loading system and pre-set meter, with (17) Quick-connect couplings. (18) Dunlop leaf-air springs, on both front steering axles. (19) Ladder from cab to roof walkway (also acts as emergency exit). (20) Fire extinguisher. (21) Adjustable, optical rear-view driving-mirror system gives driver a view of the road immediately behind the vehicle. (22) Aircraft-type, adjustable, sprung seats. (23) Wrap-around windscreen, with sliding side windows doubling as escape hatches.

KEY TO CAB: (24) Instrument cluster and gear-shift control. (25) Switch panels. (26) Front entrance to cab replaces usual side-doors. (27) Brake and accelerator pedals (no clutch).

Oshkosh is a make of truck you'll only usually spot in countries like the USA or South Africa - or where the US Armed Forces may be posted. There were three exceptions which came to Great Britain in the late 1960s and although BIJ 5727 was to cross the water prior to being converted for recovery work in England, the other two (one is 573 BRI) were saved for preservation by Ulster based Johnnie Fee. The right hand drive 6x4 units were rated for 80 tons gross operation when in service with McCormack Macnaughton of Belfast. They were equipped with a 100 ton capacity winch which was also used to lift the semi-trailer. Their 400bhp Caterpillar engine drove through a 10 speed Fuller 'box plus a four speed auxillary.

Paul Hancox's research reveals that Oshkosh built 744 of the M911 8x6 tractors for the US Army from 1976. They even offered it (without making any sales) to the British and European military in 1983 although it was badged as a Shelvoke SPV. Powered by the General Motors V8 Detroit two stroke engine of 435bhp, the 8x6 unit (with raisable second axle) weighed off around 17 tons while normal running weight with an M60 tank was around 110 tons. Top speed was said to be 45mph. While seeing service in Operation Desert Storm during the Gulf conflict, the M911 was to be replaced by the Oshkosh 8x8 M1070 of which 1,044 were ordered. The M60 battle tank is one of 4,088 built between 1959 and 1975 by the Detroit based member of the Chrysler Corporation, Tank Arsenal.

The Ergomatic style of cab was fitted to thousands of Leylands, AECs and Albions during the '60s and '70s although in their midst were one or two specials. The placing of the Mandator badge on the top centre of the grille on AMH 508H indicates that it was one of 365 similar vehicles built with AEC's legendary V8 engine. Westfield Transport became part of Pickfords in 1964 but it retained its identity because of its unique line of installation work. The Westfield ganging crew are (left to right) Colin Coupe, Horrice Evans and Joe Boycotte. Driver Charlie Gooding is about to leave this Hawick mill hauling one of Westfield's specially built 37' Dyson trailers. This AEC is recalled as being phenomenally quick, but prone to breakdown.

The AEC V8 proved more reliable - and longer living - than Leyland's gas turbine engines. The Comet was the first vehicle to be fitted with a turbine engine (it actually came from a Rover racing car) and the prototype was pictured by Geoff Meek at Leyland in June 1997. This vehicle has survived but the Shell Mex-BP six wheeler sadly hasn't. This was one of three which went to selected oil companies (the other two being Esso and Castrol) and after it's trials based at Fulham in early 1972, it was allocated to the Stanlow depot in May of that year. It was much quicker than anything else Shell had in service but fuel returns were poor. While the engine also suffered from reliability problems, the fully automatic gearbox also proved a major niggling point. It was returned to Leyland after about a year in service and subsequently the gas turbine trials were discontinued.

TURBINE~SMOOTH TRUCK

In 1966, Ford of America built an experimental gas-turbine truck. *Motor Transport* tested it. . .

DRIVING a gas turbine truck is deceptive, mainly because of its simplicity. When I drove the Ford 707 this week I was prepared for the lack of noise and the smoothness, because I had talked to Pat Kennett about his experiences with the truck in Germany (*Motor Transport*, September 12). But I did not appreciate the feeling of relaxation which this smoothness gives.

Basically, driving a gas turbine is very little different from driving a diesel. There are the same controls, and the same technique is required for gear changing. The deceptiveness comes in if you drive by ear and by feel, instead of using the instruments.

On starting away, for example, it is possible, and even desirable, to ease the clutch in with the engine running at "tick over" until the truck begins to move. Then you push down on the accelerator and glide away. I use the word glide deliberately, because there is none of the usual sudden bite and falling off in the feel of the engine that is familiar with a diesel. The lack of snatch makes manoeuvring out of a parking space particularly easy.

I took over the truck at a demonstration at the Rank motorway service centre on the M2 in Kent, and appreciated this need of crawling along when the attendant who marked out the parking area with cones did not appreciate the room required to manoeuvre a 50ft-long outfit.

Going down the access road on the motorway I was inclined to hold on to the gears too long before changing up. Subconsciously, I suppose, I was waiting for the "feel" of a diesel change-up point. I was advised by Skip Rautio, a member of Ford's turbine development team of the revolution speeds at which to change, and when these were used instead of the feel of the engine, the acceleration and smooth pick-up of the unit were marked.

Once again, the deceptiveness of the turbine showed itself in that, particularly on a motorway, the sense of acceleration could only be judged by watching the speedometer — and the speed with which I caught up with a car I had allowed to go past before I pulled off the access road.

The turbine rotors, of course, revolve much faster than a diesel engine crankshaft, and there was a turbine tachometer in the cab reading up to 50,000 revolutions a minute. But there was also an output shaft tachometer which recorded much more familiar speeds. Using this, I found the turbine required much the same driving technique as say a V8 diesel. The best change-up point was between 2,800 and 2,900 r.p.m. The engine was coupled to a normal Fuller five-speed gear box via a normal dry-plate clutch, so there was nothing unfamiliar here.

On the motorway, there was practically no difference in feel between 30 m.p.h. in fourth gear and 70 m.p.h. in top. When I wound the window down, the wind noise was more than the engine noise. With the feeling of relaxation which this quiet progress gave, I found myself driving with a smoothness of which I was conscious. Every manoeuvre or movement of the controls felt unhurried. So much so, in fact, that when I prepared to pull off the motorway onto the exit slip road I found myself doing just over 55 miles an hour. A speed of 35 m.p.h. seemed a positive crawl. It is a point which drivers will have to watch when they first take over a gas-turbine truck, but I soon became used to it, and after about an hour I felt it would not be long before I could "play it by ear." as Skip Rautio put it.

So much for driving. What about the other aspects of operating? I talked to Ivan Swatman, Ford's chief engineer for turbine operations, about operating and servicing costs. On fuel consumption he quoted specific consumption figures in pounds per b.h.p. per hour. This is fine from an engineer's point of view, but operators want figures in miles per gallon. Mr Swatman would not be drawn. But he said that when production begins and trucks are put on the market they will have "no excuse" engines.

They will be competitive in fuel consumption, ease of servicing, and durability, he said. He mentioned figures of a quarter of a million miles before attention, which he said American operators demand. On training mechanics to service gas turbines, he thought that any good fitter would have no trouble at all after a one-week conversion course. The change in technique for fitters would be no more marked than in the change from petrol to diesel years ago.

The unit in the Ford 707 truck gives 375 b.h.p. installed A 335 b.h.p. engine is imminent, and other units with outputs down to 200 b.h.p. are under development.

Mr. Swatman said that naturally Ford hoped to be first in the field with a gas turbine on the market. But the company was not going to rush into production before it had completed its extensive development programme. He hoped, for the future of gas turbine trucks, that no other manufacturers would rush into production with an under-developed unit and "foul up the market for a long time."

On price, he said that this was outside his field but, again, it would be competitive. Operators, he said, would not buy something expensive on the basis of promises in the future.

Ford of America also built and trialed a gas turbine truck which was brought across to Europe for the Press to examine. However, similar to the Leyland vehicles, this concept never reached full production.

Thornycroft built over 1,000 Antars and it seems amazing that very few ever entered the UK heavy haulage scene. The first ones had the Rover V8 petrol engine although VDN 150H was a Mark III and had the straight eight cylinder Rolls Royce diesel producing 333bhp. Elliotts actually bought three Antars although the other two petrol engined ones were purely for spares. Seen in November 1971, driver Ken Pitts is rounding York enroute from Blackpool to ICI Wilton on Teesside. The purpose built ballast box was made by Roy Atkinson from one inch thick steel plate. Roy recalls the Antar engine blew up and when the Elliotts ceased trading the vehicle was still unserviceable so it went for scrap.

King of the heavyweight special builders during the '70s and '80s was Peter Searson. The feats of his four Scammell Contractor / Volvo / Detroit or Caterpillar powered HHT hybrids saw Heanor Haulage move up the heavyweight league. SAL 513R was the second of these specials although instead of noticing the tractor, company drivers like Alan Needham will probably tell you about the Searson built semi-trailer he's hauling. The load carrier was nicknamed 'Lollapa', although no one seems to know why. Sporting two rear axles of eight tyres in line, the trailer was actually 12' wide and ideal to support crawler machines. It did prove to be a problem when empty as it took up far too much road and at times could be an embarrassment.

Scammell only built six of the Mark II Contractors. With the K range of Cummins 450 engine, many people felt the Mark II was the finest heavy haulage vehicle ever built - they were certainly powerful performers. Pickfords bought XUU 919 and 925T and the pair is seen hauling one of four 325 tonne Davy McKee castings from Doncaster to Sheffield in 1983. All up train weight was around 500 tonnes. In April 1993, Pickfords sold this pair on and they were bought to work in Thailand. One of the many incidents in the Far East was the time they went to Vietnam for a big job. The authorities there were so impressed with the big Mark IIs they decided to keep them - without paying for them. However, within about a month they had a change of heart and the Scammells were returned to their French owner.

Overleaf: I've made no secret as to my thoughts on the Mark 1 240 ton Scammell Contractor as in their time, there was nothing else to compare. Some people in the UK now reckon they're too big and unwieldy but you cannot take away their many achievements. Both Wynns and Sunters have a lot to thank them for although when the Northallerton trio of HVN 397N, LAJ 798P and YVN 308T were disposed of, the Lift & Shift concern in India soon put them back to work. The Robert Price photograph sees 'Resolute' on the A41 in March 1976, while Bill Jamieson is seen in LAJ 798P rounding the Cleveland Bay on Teesside and in the heart of Sullom Voe in the Shetlands. The trade plated unit has just left the Crane Fruehauf trailer works in Dereham enroute to Russia.

VOLVO F88/F89

It's hard to appreciate how big an impact the Volvo F88 had on the British transport scene. When it first appeared in 1967, no one had seen anything quite like it. It wasn't the first Volvo to be imported in big numbers (that mantle went to the smaller F86 - or 'Bubble' as it was sometimes nicknamed) but the impact it made was staggering. Drivers couldn't believe how quiet, smooth and powerful these new Volvos were and until the late 1970s, the truck was a bench mark that other manufacturers tried to emulate.

The F88 story begins in the late '50s when Volvo were trying to market their vehicles in the USA. That project didn't meet with much success but the development of the large tilting cab - the F88's trademark - made it's first appearance around that time. The first models into production during 1962 with the cab were the L4951 (4x2s) and L4956 (6x2 version) which were known by Volvo as the Titan Tiptop.

The Titan range was short lived as the early '60s saw Volvo involved in major development work of their drivelines. The new 9.6 litre TD100 engine was to be at the heart of the F88 (and the bonneted N88 version plus the G88 which had the front axle located further forward) together with a new eight speed, range change gearbox (four gears in a high and low range).

The vehicle's performance was enhanced after 1969 with the introduction of the gearbox splitter (allowing for 16 different gear ratios) although the UK was hardly getting to grips with this superb new truck when news of an even better one emerged.

To look at, there seems little difference between the F88 and the F89. Most people will tell you that the latter is always left hand drive (the tilted angle of its engine apparently prevented it being offered in right hand drive form - although I'm aware of one RHD conversion) but it was the power from the 330bhp 12 litre engine which placed the 89 at the top of the pile.

To appease the right hand drive UK market, Volvo tweaked the 88's engine to produce the 290bhp version and while enhancing performance, it didn't have the 240's reliability.

The F88 transformed Volvo's impact on the British market. In 1967 they sold 165 trucks but this rose to the 2,000 mark in 1972. By 1975, Volvo was the market leader in tractors with train weights over 29 tonnes. It's thus not surprising so many drivers of old have particularly fond memories of their days with the F88. What amazed many was how it was phased out of production in 1978 (and replaced by the F10/12) at a time when it was so well thought of.

As Oswald Transport of Ayr (part of the GKN Group from 1965) regularly hauled new crankshafts and axles for both Volvo and Scania out of Scottish Stampings - to Immingham docks for export - they understandably felt obliged to operate vehicles of both these marques. Bob Jamieson was to end up as Oswald's transport manager and he recalls their first F88-240 six wheelers were the well liked MAG 245G and OCS 463H. He cannot recall MCS 538G - even though it has Oswald's name on the door - and thinks it was actually allocated to another part of the GKN Group as he knows Oswald never striped their front bumper.

Peter Searson of Heanor Haulage recalls his first thoughts of the Volvo F88 were filled with trepidation. The big trouble with them, he remembered, was they were 'just like driving a car and he anticipated a mutiny amongst those company drivers who weren't allocated one. Heanor's first F88 is believed to be the pictured GHU 298K. The vehicle was bought second hand when about two years old from the Bournemouth based dealer of Ken Flowers. Peter had travelled down from Derbyshire with his father Ken and it was when he drove the vehicle back home that he realised what an excellent performer it was. Although Heanor did buy other second hand F88s through Flowers, all new Volvos were bought through the John Hebb dealership at Wootton near Immingham. They included six F89 4x2s, similar to LFU 917R which is seen in the Terry Agland photograph (top). The F89 is recalled by Peter as being particularly strong and he says it was capable of taking a 27 tonnes loading through its drive axle. In typical Heanor fashion, all the trailers on show are slightly different. SRB 612M is coupled to a 45' long Boden with wide spread axles while GHU 334K is hauling a tri-axle Boden. Supporting the end of the 90' long Butterly crane girder is a four in line bogie which started life in a military Taskers built trailer.

The F88 range covered both four and six wheeled articulated tractor units and rigids - although the latter were rarely seen in the UK at least. Kenny Rutherford first began in haulage during the mid '60s as a clearing house based in Bridgegate House in Irvine. He eventually went on to operate his own small fleet and this F88-240 is believed to have been used to haul nylon produce for the Chemstrand concern. The immediate identifying factor of what engine an F88 is fitted with is usually given by the size of the vehicle's front grille. The 240 had the smaller one while the later 290s had the full width grille.

Sunters of Northallerton thought highly of their F89 HVN 396N which they rated as good for payloads up to the 80-90 ton mark while its purpose built ballast box certainly enhanced its looks. With timber frame and light alloy panels, the box was built by the Watkinson Coachbuilding firm of Northallerton. Specialists in making horse boxes and the like (the company now trades under the JSW title) this was the third similar ballast box made for Sunters. The other vehicles were the six wheeler Atkinsons PAJ 50 and NPY 63F. Pictured leaving Head Wrightsons on Teesside, this Volvo usually had Malcolm Johnson as its driver. Jim Hacking of Horwich near Bolton was to buy this F89 in February 1993 but rather than pension it off, Jim used it for general haulage to the Middle and Far East. It's pictured by Jim in Saudi Arabia during March 1996.

AV Dawson of Middlesbrough is another operator who thought well of their F88s. HEF 7N usually had Dave Lupton as its driver and was said to be good for low loader work up to around 120 tons gross. It's pictured with a 75' long Crane Fruehauf rear steer grossing something like 57 tons with George Elliott as driver. In a previous career, I was almost on first name terms with many drivers - and operators - of the heavier vehicles on the road. However, if you wish to upset Maurice Dawson just show him this photograph and mention my name. We begged to disagree over several points in shot - and he still can recall them over 20 years later. Stan Towler, a manager at Dawsons, may also tell you the story about why he was dragged off his sick bed when this photograph was being taken. Although the F88 was sold (believedly to BSC) the semi-trailer is still in use by Dawsons.

Ian Crawshaw recalls KFU 513P as only capable of a 45mph top speed although the low speed diffs did allow this F88 to gross up to 100 tons. Ian is pictured steering the rear bogie as driver Jock Hall inches back into Farringdon Street Underground station in this James Dixon photograph. The 30 ton of Grant Lyon 30 shunting locomotive was only used here for a short time before it was re-loaded and taken back to Scunthorpe. TSL's other F88 6x4 was JJV 587P which Pete Glover usually drove. This latter unit wasn't geared down and could thus reach 60mph. TSL was to be absorbed into the VVS Group of Leeds although the TSL livery has recently been brought back into use.

When Sparrows Crane Hire put this F89 6x4 LFB 887P on the road in 1976, it's believed to have been the only tower rig crane of its type in Europe. Although it has Bath written on the door, the outfit operated out of the company's Colnbrook depot near London. The 27 ton capacity tower crane was manufactured by GCI, General Crane Industries of London, Ontario, Canada and is pictured by the Bristol workshops manager John Frost as it underwent checking prior to going into service. The rearmost three axles supporting the crane were hydraulically steered via sensors detecting movement through the Volvo's fifth wheel. The Sparrow business was operated by the three Sparrow brothers Gordon, George and Alf although it was bought by the BET Group in the 1980s and merged to form the large concern of Grayston, White and Sparrow.

Geoff Cook's first experience with the F88s was when he was running the Siddle C Cook concern at Consett. The model was so well liked that when he set up Elddis Transport in 1971 he invested heavily in them. Elddis Fleet Engineer Michael Sullivan recalls the firm ran about 22 of these 4x2s on UK general haulage work - a large number hauling Crane Fruehauf dry freight van trailers. Michael recalls the camshaft on the 290 version wasn't strong enough to take the extra torque (when compared to the 240s) and all the Elddis F88s had to be modified. This Roger Kenny shot recalls that by 1976, Elddis had taken their 84th vehicle into service.

If ever there was a competition for the longest living / hardest worked F88 240 then Bob Baron's SCB 170K must be a winner. Still in active service in 1999 (albeit downplated to 26 tonnes for fork lift haulage) the vehicle was new to Premier Plant at Blackburn in 1972. Bob paid £4,600 for it in 1976 and it's worked almost non stop since then. It's pictured by Dave Weston (with Bob at the wheel) after he'd reversed back to this low bridge in Nelson. The only question Bob couldn't answer was how long SCB would continue earning its keep.

Tom Shanks of Aberdeen was another big fan of the F88 and he continued to use several of them in the early 1990s mainly on local oil related work but also on regular trips to Glasgow: 'I liked them - and so did the drivers,' he said. GNV 225N was bought about 1990 from an owner driver in the Northampton area while MSA 502P started life on tanker work with William Nicol's. The strangest Shanks F88 story relates to LPV 440V. The 240 unit was bought new in 1972 by the Massey Ferguson dealer Barclay Brothers of Bury St Edmunds. It went into storage for eight years and was first registered in 1980. It did very little work and when Tom bought the 4x2 unit, it had only covered 2,000 kilometres. He re-registered it DRS 67K and when he ceased trading around 1995 it only had some 30,000kms on the clock. He was to sell this lightly used Volvo to Riddle of Glenkiddle. The 290 powered GNV 225N was also sold on and it did livestock work before Mandy Stewart bought it for her husband Jim as a surprise birthday present. The Stewarts - who manufacture agricultural trailers from their base near Inverurie - are used to strange acts like this as a friend gave them an old Scania 111 as a wedding present.

Paddy Conroy and Brian Burgess are the two who joined forces in 1974 to create C&B haulage. During the 1980s, the pair were to get tremendous service from eight second hand F88s. Their first one was the ex Dawson Rentals WJO 700R which cost £12,000 at auction. NAF 373R was usually driven by Brian's son Graham and cost only £4,0000. Bought from an owner driver at Bracknell, it started life with English China Clay in Cornwall. Paddy & Brian still rave about the exploits of their F88s: 'It had too good a heater,' recalled Brian, 'in fact one of ours caught fire on the Aachen border.' Although NAF has long since been cut up, the York tandem axle tilt trailer (converted by CF into a tri-axle curtainsider) is still at C&B.

SCAMMELL CRUSADER

Going through the 60 years of archives illustrating Scammell production, I found it very difficult to select only one model to specifically highlight as the Watford manufacturer produced many candidates for inclusion in a book of this nature.

While some purists may argue because it hasn't got an exposed bonnet it isn't a true Scammell, to me the Crusader range of tractor units was something special. Even now, 20 years after the model went out of production in 1979, their huge daunting presence can still evoke all sorts of emotions. Whether you loved or hated them was a personal choice - their distinctive makeup meant you could hardly ignore them.

The story of the Crusader began in the mid 1960s. Although 1965 had just seen the maximum permitted weight limits rise from 24 to 32 tons, there were still rumours that a further rise to 38, 40 or even 44 tons would be permitted for artics - provided a double drive six wheeled tractor unit was used. Yes, although many new models usually start with a four wheeled unit and then evolve to a six wheeler, the Crusader range was to make that move in reverse.

As well as requiring inbuilt strength for a potentially higher weight capacity (something which has been a Scammell trait for almost their entire production) the other main concepts for the

MUR 501H was a prototype of the new 6x4 range and this photograph was to grace many of the early Crusader brochures. The shot was taken on its first testing run when Howard Barnes drove it overland from Watford to Tehran, the capital of Iran. The journey was a regular haul done by Asian Transport and they were to provide the fully loaded trailer (the container was apparently loaded with a mix of Gillette razor blades and whisky - all of which were safely delivered). In the late 1960s Howard was a development engineer at Scammells (he's now a director with Alvis Unipower) and was very much involved in the Crusader's creation. After Scammell had finished with this unit, it's believed to have been sold to a circus operator who used it to haul elephants.

new range was it had to be quick across the ground - something which Scammells were usually not known for - while also requiring minimum maintenance.

To produce this Utopian form of flying machine meant the Scammell design team had to start from scratch. The company's historic driveline formulae for general haulage vehicles had been a Gardner (or perhaps Leyland) engine plus distinctive Scammell gated gearbox driving to their cylindrically shaped rear axle. However in plumping for a GM V8-71 Series Detroit two stroke diesel engine coupled to a 15 speed Fuller gearbox, Scammells opted for something almost unknown in the UK yet was a proven combination in the USA.

Historians will note this isn't the first time Scammells have taken inspiration from our

American cousins as those first Watford built artics back in 1922 were produced after seeing the Knox variant of the same outfit.

Although the 'Jimmy' two stroke engine was to champion the Crusader around the world, it wasn't apparently the first engine option to be thought of. When the new model was being conceived, the 272bhp AEC V8 four stroke was seriously considered and it's believed a prototype was tried with this form of power pack. It's reported that AEC were also planning to produce their own form of Crusader style of Supertruck although both the idea and the use of the phenomenally powerful engine were soon dropped.

LRA 435J was exhibited at the Earl's Court Show in 1970 and was the first of five similar Detroit powered 6x4 Crusaders bought by Peter Searson's company Heanor Haulage. Neil Bennett driving and Walter Boyko as mate, the Scammell's carrying 40 tonnes of Aveling Barford dumper from Grantham. The weight's been taken on trailer no. 74, a King tandem axle low loader which Heanor got excellent service from. Although very pleased to see the 6x4 Crusader's arrival as a lightweight heavy hauler, what Peter Searson really wanted was a large number of Detroit powered 4x2 Crusader tractor units. He only received one and when Scammell told him he'd have to have any others with Rolls Royce engines, he decided to take his business elsewhere.

VNO 4L came into service with C J Pryor of Harlow during mid 1972 and was given new to long serving driver George Murray (on 31.12.98 he'd clocked up 51 years with the firm). The combination is seen collecting a D8 Caterpillar 68A which weighed something like 33 tonnes. George recalls the 6x4 Crusader was a replacement for an AEC Mammoth Major six wheeled unit and when compared to that old motor was reckoned as 'brilliant'. George had started with Pryors in 1947 when their sole motor was an ex Army AEC Matador and the company was then involved in round timber work. In 1999, the business is still family owned but they're now one of the biggest privately owned earth moving concerns in Essex. While VNO was well capable of living up to its potential, George recalled you had to keep the Detroit two stroke revs up to produce the power. This Scammell only stayed with Pryors for about three years as a very good deal prompted a trade in for another new 6x4 Crusader in early '76.

Not many UK road hauliers may have had knowledge of the Detroit although the American marque of engine had a 30 year track record which perhaps was best known for applications throughout the construction industry. First rated to produce 287bhp at 2,100rpm may seem fairly modest in 1999 but 30 years earlier it was producing more than 100bhp above the standard workhorse of the day - the Gardner 6LXB-180.

Scammell had first offered the Fuller 15 speed 'box in some lightweight versions of their heavy haulage Contractor range (introduced in 1964) so this part of the transmission wasn't a total unknown. A high and low range of five gears was supplemented by a deep reduction choice of five lower gears which gave the Crusader the potential to weather all sorts of gut stumping conditions.

I must admit a bias towards Fuller equipment and while the latest technology may have gone beyond this traditional box of cogs, in many other people's eyes they haven't improved on the Fuller's lightening gearshifts and long term reliability.

To put the power onto the road, Scammell's first version of drive axles appeared similar to those used on the Albion Reiver. Known as lightweights, they were subsequently replaced in the 44 and 65 ton gross tractors with the heavier Maudslay version. Known as Group axles, this manufacturing part of the Leyland Empire was later to pass to Rubery Owen - Rockwell.

One thing which hardly altered throughout the Crusader's life was it's cab. True you could have either a day or sleeper version of the solid looking (brick shed like) steel construction made by Motor Panels but that was it. Built specifically not to tilt - a decision that Scammell would later question -

the reasoning being as the V8 engine was standard, a tilting cab might partially block access to the front part of the engine where most of the auxiliaries were situated.

Never questioned was the choice of name for the the new model. Michael Knowles lays claim to suggesting this title as he says he first thought of it in 1962. Then a rather young engineer in the making, he'd apparently built a six wheeled model out of Meccano and sent photos to Scammell suggesting the design (which he named Crusader) as a possible new model.

His correspondence was acknowledged by the then publicity manager Mr P F Woods and although the design wasn't followed up, Michael did gain employment at Watford in the late '60s and was involved in the works design team. When the subject of what to name the new model came up, Michael re-suggested his title of Crusader and as it had a clean, solid sound to it, the Knowles idea was adopted.

No matter what you call a vehicle, it's destiny is decided on how good it does its job. The first long haul for the prototype MUR 501H was to the Iranian capital of Tehran and back. With that safely under its belt, the rest of the industry began seriously looking at the latest model to bear the Scammell name.

Although Pickfords had long been Scammell users (and were to get extended service from many 6x4 Crusaders) the general haulage division of British Road Services had never bought many Scammells. However high performance, minimal maintenance and proven reliability were factors which made the BRS engineers sit up and although they weren't interested in the 6x4s, they

W A Glendinning were never big Scammell users although a competitive price prompted the purchase of HNL 969L through the Hargreaves dealership at Stockton. While director Ken Glendinning recalls he liked the maintenance free suspension, the 4x2's Rolls Royce engine did suffer from problems because of its wet liner construction. Good service from this Crusader prompted Glendinnings to buy two new 'M' reg units although HNL did suffer from more accidents than most vehicles. One freak incident was when a vehicle heading the other way shed its spare wheel and getting lodged under the Crusader caused it to veer off the road and turn over. 'Jam Jar' was the nickname of top general haulage driver Davy Johnson who came to the firm after Archie Glendinning had bought out the Ryton based firm he was working for of W Dance.

It seems impossible that there'd be a strong link between the impressive line up of Crusaders operated by Sam Williamson (top) - who was based in New Zealand - and the example operated by the British Army (bottom). Sam apparently felt so strongly about the Crusaders that he almost had a love affair with them as he said they were almost ideal for his logging work. His well turned out fleet was such a fine advertisement for the model that when the UK Ministry of Defence were considering buying this class of machine, the request to see and meet an operator in the field took them to the Williamson place on Landscape Road, Te-puke, Bay of Plenty in the North Island. The glowing Williamson reference prompted a big investment in 4x2s (for the Royal Corps of Transport) and 6x4 65 tonners to the Royal Engineers. The 6x4 was also kitted out with Swedish ECKA equipment and used by the REME for recovery purposes.

felt a 4x2 version may fit well into their fleet requirements.

Walter Batstone was the BRS Group's Engineering Advisor in the late 1960s and he was quoted as being aptly proud of its association in the design and development of the Crusader 4x2. He was at pains to point out that many BRS drivers, fitters, workshops engineers and designers all had input into the final details of the vehicle.

The cab may not have changed although the four wheelers were to take the Rolls Royce Eagle six cylinder engine as standard either in 220bhp (naturally aspirated) or 280bhp (turbocharged) form. While the drive axle was from the long established heavyweight Leyland Beaver, the gearbox was either a 10 or 9 speed Fuller with a 17" single or 15" twin plate clutch respectively.

The new 4x2s were built to operate at the UK maximum of 32 tons although export versions were plated for either 34 tons (with the 220 engine) or 40 tons with the bigger 280. It was thus apparent that the rating of 38 (or 44) tons for the original 6x4s was fairly modest so a re-assessment was done to change their ratings to either 50 or 65 tons.

In fairness, Scammell engineers didn't seem to have a clue as to how strong their vehicles were - although many operators soon realised. In my earlier days in law enforcement I can recall a junior officer asking advice on what weight I thought a particular low loader was he had stopped. The paperwork produced by the driver gave the notified weight as 63 tons - although it was known for errors to be made in this domain.

In deciding to weigh the outfit off, we selected a weighbridge close to where he was due to deliver so we escorted him about 20 miles to this point. The Detroit powered 6x4 Scammell had travelled from the south coast near Brighton and made easy progress to Hartlepool in fact it was that easy I thought he would be under his declared weight. It was a surpise to me - but perhaps not to the driver - that when he drove onto the British Steel scales, the weighbridge indicated he was actually grossing 95 tons. Yes 30 tons above the weight which Scammell said he shouldn't exceed.

It's thus not surprising when Scammell produced the Samson - an eight wheeled version of the Crusader - they had no takers, as they only rated this for 75 tons gross even though the original did give Pickfords - and later owner Tony Kimber - good service.

Less reliable was those early Rolls Royce engines. Being of wet liner construction (water flowed round the outside of the cylinder) meant they suffered from the effects of electrolysis. This wasn't just a problem for the Rollers as all wet liner engines would see pitting in the bores which allowed water to pass through into the cylinders.

Going into service for the Assam State Electricity Board in India prior to September 1981 were seven mobile generating stations built by Ruston Gas Turbines of Lincoln. Each station consisted of a gas turbine generating set, a control / switchgear unit and a turbine fuel gas compression unit. In addition, three extra trailer mounted transformer units were supplied to step up the power from 11,000 to 33,000 volts. The value of the order was in excess of £6m although Ruston had supplied similar generating sets to Argentina and Saudi Arabia. Eight Scammell Crusaders - complete with hydraulic winches - moved the 24 trailers of equipment which incorporated goose necks and a steerable rear bogie built by King Trailers.

Liner cracking and sealing ring failure could also be a headache.

The symptoms to the defect were of the engine not being able to start on a morning (cylinder full of water) or of getting hot too easily. Rolls Royce worked quickly on the problem and they soon found that running all year on a 50/50 mix of water and anti-freeze would eliminate the problem and the engine would run for years.

Another problem relating to over heating was how such an occurrence would inevitably prompt a valve seat to drop. Hauliers like Maurice Sissons of Sherburn-in-Elmet (who became a Crusader devotee) knew that if a driver ever reported an engine getting too hot, the vehicle was immediately brought in and the cylinder heads removed for inspection. Rolls Royce were to also

work on this problem and subsequently put a lip over the valve seat so it couldn't drop.

Water - and its temperature - was a major problem with early Crusaders and this was aggravated with teething problems over the model's famous swinging radiator. Having a fixed cab, the Scammell design team had come up with the brilliant concept of having a hinging front grille and radiator. It was like opening a pair of double doors for in seconds you had access to the fan belt, alternator and water pump. The idea was good although there were problems with the first type of convoluted water hoses because of age hardening and cracking.

How operators came to terms with the Crusader's difficulties varied in the extreme. Exports of the model went as far as South and

International Transport & Contracting (ITC) had a big fleet of Crusaders which were operated up to 65 tons gross. One problem with the GM two stroke in places like Zimbabwe, Sudan and Saudi Arabia was with the high sulphur content of the local fuel. In bad conditions it meant the engine needed re-ringing every 50,000 miles. Some hauliers discovered the two stroke engine ran better on kerosene so the likes of Esso Blue and Fina Green paraffin were made use of in place of conventional diesel. Scammell field engineer Geoff Clarke made regular visits to ITC to monitor the sulphur problem and he recalls the test route of a fully freighted 65 tonner was up the infamous 15 mile long Taif escarpment out of Jeddah. At the steepest point, the Crusaders required the lowest cog in the 15 speed box.

Central Africa, Australia and New Zealand, it being shipped out from Watford in kit form for local assembly. The cab went in partially knocked down form as in Australia a far better interior trim was desired to the standard UK version - although in Zimbabwe, there were complaints that the Crusader was too sophisticated for local drivers.

One big user of the Crusader in this country was Heinz Herman who had apparently replaced all his old AECs with 6x4 Scammells on a ratio of one Crusader for two AECs. Known as Herman the German, he worked his Detroit powered machines very hard although when the Scammell field men went to see the Crusaders in action, they came back with some strange stories.

Perhaps the strangest sight which field engineer Geoff Clarke ever saw was not an African based Crusader but an old Scammell Handyman III. Its owner driver originated from Hull but he'd driven his Gardner 180 powered Scammell overland and was making a living in Saudia Arabia. His regular route was over the infamous Taif escarpment which at 15 miles long was a Middle East version of the old climbs up Shap, Beattock and Drummosie Brae (near Inverness) all rolled into one - and rather hotter.

One thing that old Scammell didn't have, was an extra fitted to the Crusader to try and limit the damage caused by overheating. The temperature and low level indicator - TALLI - lit up a dashboard light when the water got too hot or the level dropped too far. Sadly this didn't work very well as either the light stayed on all the time or didn't come on at all, never mind the state of the water.

Glynn Rees, now with the Unipower concern, recalled that Heinz Herman solved this problem by plumbing the overflow of the radiator to a point just above the accelerator pedal. So when the water did boil, the excess travelled along the pipe and dropped onto the driver's right foot. True it almost scalded him but it indicated rather vividly that he had to stop and check the water.

The Herman fleet was ran particularly fast and when visitors from Watford jumped aboard, it was almost with an air of nervousness. Heading for South Africa fully freighted, the long drop down the escarpment saw selection of 'silent 16th', as coasting in neutral was almost a way of life.

I reckoned that the Herman drivers must have been given lessons by Scammell service engineer Bob Willoughby. While never saying he drives like a maniac (he might sue me) my ride with him through the streets of Teesside in Newcastle Airport's Scammell crash tender Fire 5, will never be forgotten.

At times, the Herman vehicles did come to grief although Heinz's rebuilds were also worth a look. He reckoned that as none of his drivers could read, fitting anything more than basic instrumentation was trivia. All his drivers needed was a seat, a steering wheel, three pedals to press and perhaps a row of warning lights indicating when there was a problem with air, water, oil or electrics. His point may have had an element of truth to it as Crusaders assembled in Kenya are recalled as having an excellent paint quality but also for usually having their gauges inserted upside down - as the fitters couldn't read either.

The Crusader gained a fine reputation in New Zealand especially with operators like Sam Williamson - although not necessarily with Sam's wife. Apparently Sam was the sort of guy who would prefer to buy a new Crusader rather than the new kitchen his wife wanted.

Sam found the latest Scammell ideal for his logging work although the NZ versions of the Crusader were often quite different from their UK counterparts. The usual kit for a new vehicle often contained the 'Samson' length of chassis rails and even though not everyone was an eight wheeler, they did have a wide variety of wheelbases.

One design of the standard Crusader spec' which was liked throughout the globe was the Crusader's suspension. The radical design used semi-elliptic leaf springs mounted above the axle with their front and rear couplings to the vehicle chassis done in such a fashion to totally eliminate lubrication.

The rear ends of the spring were in slipper type mountings i.e. simply held in place by their own weight and allowed to slide in and out in line with axle/chassis movements. The case hardend wearing surfaces on the mountings were just discarded once they became worn through - or in some cases, operators just turned them round to wear down the other 50% which wasn't worn with the original movement.

The front end of the spring was located in bonded rubber bushes (which didn't require any greasing) but the bracket was so designed that when the bush needed changing, a couple of nuts were removed and the bracket split in half. Never had a fitter's life been so easy - or so the designers hoped.

The next step for the design team was in creating an even stronger Crusader. The 100 tons gross version was built specifically at the request of Wynns Heavy Haulage. Their head engineer Stan Anderson suggested the Scammell would be capable of taking the extra weight if a Contractor double drive rear bogie was put into a Crusader chassis.

Mick Green who rose to be Sales Contract Manager with Scammells between 1978 and 1983 recalls he and his wife Helen drew up a list of about 12 names - one of which was 'Amazon'. This was adopted for this new breed of Crusader but

While most Scammell followers are aware there was only one eight wheeled Scammell Samson (originally EYF 866J but later Q362 NTR) it's not to say there was only one eight wheeled Scammell Crusader. Australia and New Zealand had all sorts of variants at work - similar to the Western Haulage vehicle - as Crusaders were shipped out in kit form but always having overlength chassis rails so they could be cut to any size required. In the North East of England Dave Metcalfe and Alan Sewell built the 8x4 Q874 DAJ by adding a second steering axle to an ex army 6x4 65 tonner. Kitted out with all manner of recovery gear (most of it transplanted from an ex military Leyland Martian) 'Fearnought Retriever' tips the scales at 26 tons but has lived up to its evocative name recovering all shapes and sizes from all sorts of situations. Painted in Shamara Heavy Haulage colours, the Samson was brought back to life in 1983 when owner Tony Kimber rescued it from a decaying death in a Southampton dealer's yard. Main job for the 8x4 Scammell in the mid '80s was as a pushing tractor to a specially built cable carrying trailer of Pirellis. However Tony recalls that when the leading Scammell Contractor had a fuel problem, the Samson was strong enough to push the empty outfit to the factory even though all up weight was 140 tons. Not bad for a vehicle rated to only gross 75 tons.

one other name which never made the step beyond the specification sheet was for the 150 tons version entitled 'Goliath'. Transmission for that vehicle was based on a Spicer 10 speed gearbox and Brockhouse torque convertor as plans (dated 21.2.78) were put on hold until the S24 and S26 ranges were unveiled in the early 1980s.

It must be stressed that the Crusader was by no means perfect. Those early Detroit engines were known for their noise and their thirst for fuel. The Fuller gearbox would rattle on tickover like a bag of hammers and when the Kysor radiator shutters were wide open, the passage of air made such a distinctive whistle. It made you imagine you were driving a pre war Mercedes car with a Supercharger or at the controls of a jet aircraft coming into land.

There were problems with the air intakes which had to be routed away from the exhaust and also with the lubrication of the hub on the four wheeled version. Haulier Maurice Sissons recalls that it was an apprentice's job every Friday to pull the bung out and top up every nearside hub as the oil tended to work up the halfshaft and disappear into the differential.

But to men who worked and loved this Classic from Watford, these weren't problems but simply idiosyncrasies of a vehicle which gave sterling service.

One of the strangest looking Scammell Crusaders was NSU 628P which in 1983 was the pride and joy of Cirencester based Bond Trucking. Brothers Alan, Geoff and Clive Bond spent about a year transforming a standard 220 Rolls powered 4x2 into a Kenworth KC100 look alike. Alan Bond has an unashamed passion for the American trucking scene thus the transformation of the Crusader. Bought cheaply from Baileys of Westbury (its reg denotes a Glasgow birth), the Scammell allowed Alan to move from his tipping business into general haulage work. The stones of granite were a sub contracted load from Total Transport and took Alan from their source - in a stone quarry on the top of Bodmin Moor - to a snow covered delivery point in Aberdeen. After using the Scammell for about nine months, Alan sold it to Jearide Ltd of Ferndown in Dorset.

Although British Road Services were strongly involved in the creation of the 4x2 Crusader, not every depot was allocated them. The vehicles were usually given to a few depots in larger numbers - rather than to every depot in smaller lots - to ease the individual depot workshop worries of maintaining a huge variety of vehicles. Guildford depot manager was John Smith who recalled they had 13 Crusaders which were generally well liked by the drivers because of their high power to weight ratio. Not liked however, was the fixed cab that made engine work so awkward. VBV 662V was one of the last to go into service at North Western BRS, it being worked out of Preston as a double shifted trunk motor.

Manufactured in 1979 but not registered until 1983, SON 26Y was apparently used by Scammell as a motor show exhibit before being bought by Peter Court at Banbury. Storrington Contractors of Sittingbourne in Kent were the next owners but when Roger Mortimore bought it in 1989, it was destined for quite a life. It's pictured in the early '90s moving a 120' long crane support beam internally in the newly constructed Thames Port Container Terminal on the Isle of Grain. Not a lot of weight here however, if you want to know the story of how it moved - completely unassisted - all of 1,000 tons then you'll have to ask Roger. He swears it's not simply a fisherman's tale. Although he sold his heavy haulage business in late 1998, the much cherished Detroit powered Crusader was not part of the transaction.

If ever you want to know how strong the Scammell Amazon is then have a word with father & son, Vic and Kevin Cooke. Based at Beccles in Suffolk, their diverse fleet includes A164 GGV (chassis no.63187) which was one of the last Amazons to be sold. As it was then an out of date model, it only cost the haulier £23,575 which was half the original list price. It also came with a design rating for 130 tonnes gross operation. In October 1996, the Scammell - driven by Graham Woods - moved this massive Norfolk Line bridging pontoon into storage at Great Yarmouth docks. True the distance involved was only 500 yards but the all up weight was around 190 tonnes. A Transquip four axle low loader and a pair of solid tyred trailers took the weight.

Q979 FLE is not so much a Scammell Crusader but more an Attlee Animal. The 18 tonnes of vehicle is the pride and joy of Earl Attlee (known as John to his friends) who ran a London based recovery operation before he got more involved in the House of Lords. Most of the 6x6 is a Scammell Constructor but as John wanted a decent crew cab on the vehicle, he decided to transplant a large proportion of an 'L' reg Crusader's front end. The engine / gearbox is a Rolls Royce 290 coupled to a nine speed Fuller, although the original Constructor transposing box had to be seriously modified to take the new driveline. John admits that he loves the way the Animal would literally sit down before pulling away when under heavy load. The biggest job he could recall was when an 80 tonnes mobile crane of Baldwins needed recovery. This job was made easier only when a baby alarm was used as an intercom between the crane and the Scammell.

ATKINSON BORDERER

The Atkinson Borderer was the end of an era. Yes, it was the last Atky four wheeled tractor unit to be made before the merger into Seddon Atkinson, but really it was the last of its kind of true blue, traditional British lorries.

Good riddance you'd think some people might say and while there are plenty old drivers who may have no wish to ever drive one again, there were many hauliers who suffered withdrawal symptoms when they finally faded away. To them, the long running combination of Gardner engine, David Brown or Fuller gearbox and Kirkstall axle was so proven and sweet running, they didn't want to change.

But instead, the new Sed Atk 400 Series brought the headache of the group axle and then industrial dandruff (rust) from the all steel tilt cab. The GRP cabs on the old Borderers wouldn't tilt but they'd never corrode although the motor did have its quirks (just why did Atkinson prefer those sticky lock actuators to conventional spring brakes?)

Although the name Borderer is used generally to describe all Atky 4x2 tractors with the wrap round style of cab, the purists will cringe at such an approach. The shape of the cab dates from 1958 when it was called the Mark 1 while it was enlarged slightly in '68 to become the Mark II. The name Borderer was only coined in May 1970 (by Atkinson publicity manager Frank Whalley) as one of six different names used to identify specific models then in production.

Something like 4000 Borderers were made with a variety of engines the last one believed to be KAM 335P dating from 1975.

Gibbs of Fraserburgh never operated a massive fleet you just seemed to see their long distance roamers all over the place. The Atkinson marque was a company favourite during the '60s and '70s and they were to buy 19 Borderers in total. SAV 555K ('Knight of the Road') was the first one into service in August 1971 while the last one was LRS 461P - 'Flower of Scotland' which came new in March 1975. VAV 240L - 'The Challanger' - was the first Borderer to come with the eight cylinder Gardner engine. Gardners were preferred at Gibbs although the haulier was obliged to also take Cummins powered units. 'Gay Gordon' had Stevie Smith as one of its drivers and it's seen with one of three very light Fromco semi-trailers. Originally this Atky didn't have power steering and it received an Airomatic conversion. This wasn't the best idea as it had a stop/start method of assistance.

TTB 90M was usually driven by Norman Holland of Darwen, a long serving company driver who Tom Riding described as: 'A brilliant bloke.' This 250 Cummins powered unit had the David Brown eight speed gearbox ('They weren't a success,' said Tom) although apart from posing for this photograph, it never pulled this Crane Fruehauf 1450 cu.ft powder tank. Tom Riding waxes lyrical over the Borderer: 'They were a fantastic motor. Their simplicity of build meant our mechanics could almost maintain them in their sleep.' Ridings used to buy a lot of second hand Atkinsons - often 18 month old insurance write offs - which the garage team would rebuild or refurbish. RTB 130M was the first to be fitted with a small sleeper cab by Fowlers of Leyland. However, when they studied how it had been made, the Ridings staff reckoned they could make one better. In total, something like 200 sleeper cab pods were made by this haulier and having a one piece roof moulding meant they fought off the elements better than say the original Boalloy conversion.

Chris Bennett didn't set up in haulage until 1976 but he recalls the Borderer with some great affection. In total he bought seven second hand 4x2s - predominantly with Cummins engines - NTU 592L being the only one with the Gardner 180. Pictured by Carl Jarman, this unit cost Chris £1,000 when bought from the Stockport haulier of JC Brindley. Les Eardley was its usual driver. No matter what age, the Bennett motors were expected to pull their weight although Chris recalled that the rear axle on his Borderers proved to be a problem, once the gross weight topped 32 tons.

Suttons driver Tony Brown recalls in 1977 RDJ 279L was being driven by Billy Baxendale on the night trunk between St Helens, the London depot at Bethnal Green and back to St Helens. Suttons first Borderers were believed to be PDJ 128L (based at Durham and driven by night man Tug Wilson) and the Manchester based PDJ 130L which Jimmy McKennas drove. These two had the Gardner 180 engine as did the ex Lancashire Tar Distiller VTD 625H which Tony drove. He reckoned the 240 pulled better than the 180 on the hills and was also capable of 65mph. Suttons last three Borderers were JTB 880, 885 and 888P - all of which had the eight cylinder Gardner 240. Paul Edwards of Erith in Kent is a well known sight on the preservation scene with 885P.

Wisharts of Kirkcaldy bought out the AC Horton concern around 1964 primarily for its 'A' licences. They kept the business going although this Borderer was registered in Fife and worked out of Kirkcaldy. Although long time Atkinson users, the mid '70s saw the first Scanias came into service and these were found to be far superior to the old Atky. One bonus to having two companies was when Wisharts went into International work. With the relevant permits being issued per company, Wisharts were able to double their quota.

In 1974, Monkhouses of Longtown weren't too interested in the Sed Atk 400 Series, instead they preferred to buy two new Borderers GHH 300N and GFV 397N. Pictured by Geoff Milne at the Longtown depot, 'Dernancourt' was first driven by big Willie Veevers. Monkhouses bought these units direct through Atkinson although you'll have to ask Ian Monkhouse the story of how this one has a Blackpool registration - he wouldn't let me print it. Both the Borderers had the Cummins 250 engine and Fuller nine speed box. The only trouble they gave was with their respective rear axles, a Group version and a Kirkstall: 'I used to go to bed having nightmares about their back hub oil seals,' recalled Ian. He was to replace both axles with Eaton made ones. In mid '99, the remains of both these Atkys were still in the Monkhouse graveyard.

Pollocks were another big user of Borderers although CSC 99L is believed to be their only one with the Gardner 240 engine. Robert Doig was its regular driver and although he's now an experienced owner driver specialising on Continental work, the story goes that the first time Robert took the Atky to Holland they both ended up in a canal. While the fate of CSC isn't known, the name of 'Braw Scot' is currently attached to USA 796S, the ex Reids of Insch Borderer which has been preserved in Pollocks colours.

The Grose family first began in haulage with the horse & cart while Nick Grose's first Atkinsons came in the 1960s. Retired Grose driver Eric Davies recalled they had a fleet of Borderers although this Rick Ferrari shot of HAF 375N (usually driven by Joe Gill) illustrates the only one in service with a 150 Gardner engine: 'It had a splitter box,' recalled Eric, 'and could go as good as a 180.' Grose used tippers to haul china clay north out of Cornwall and back load with coal or grain. Eric said some of the Borderers had a 'Bird Cage' added (sleeper pod) although the lack of a night heater meant you had to run the engine at times - just to keep warm - but then almost choked on the Gardner fumes.

LEYLAND MARATHON

The early 1970s was a time when UK truck makers were gradually losing market share (both here and abroad) to Continental manufacturers. The headline grabbing, tall cab'd premium vehicles then in vogue included the Volvo F88 and Scania 110/140.

At the time, Leyland had nothing to compare. Their modest offerings were limited to the Buffalo or the similar Ergomatic cab'd AEC Mandator. However in August 1973, they shook the industry with the announcement of the Marathon range of 4x2 and 6x4 rigids & tractor units. Although then limited to 32 tons gross operation in the UK, the Marathons were designed with 44 tonnes operation in mind.

To save time and money, the Marathon was built using parts already used elsewhere in the Group. At first, the Leyland engineers considered a version of the Motor Panels cab being used on the new Crusader range, but after a presentation by GKN Sankey, they adopted a re-worked version of the standard Leyland / AEC / Albion Ergomatic cab. To allow for larger engines - and cross cab access - the cab was lifted 18" higher than normal.

While operators also had a choice of either Cummins or Rolls Royce engines, the standard Marathon power pack was the newly developed Leyland 12.47 litre TL12 producing 273bhp at 2,200rpm.

One thing that high reving engine produced was a phenomenal performance. Virtually every driver and operator who had their hands on a Marathon found it was particularly quick across the ground. However, the vehicle lost favour through questionable reliability linked to poor backup.

This period of the 1970s saw the Leyland Empire undergo all sorts of problems although none directly connected with the Marathon. The model did suffer when parts weren't available and it wasn't unusual to hear of a unit being stood - for weeks - because something like a door handle couldn't be obtained.

At the 1977 Scottish Motor Show, Leyland unveiled the revised version of Marathon 2 which in many people's eyes was a far better prospect. In a comparative road test against the brand new Volvo F10, the Marathon 2 was found to be quarter of a ton lighter, two miles per hour faster round the two day test route, a clear one mile per gallon better on fuel and £1,440 cheaper to buy. Even with all that in its favour, the tall Leyland lacked image and the Marathon 2 was shortlived as the all new T45 Roadtrain was introduced in 1979.

The Marathon existence may have been brief but it was certainly memorable - to me at least. Thanks to owner driver Ken Walton (who lived to tell the tale) I cut my HGV driving teeth on his Rolls Royce 265 powered Marathon 2 and learned to love both it and its superb Fuller gearbox.

GBT 325N was new to Bright Steels Transport of Malton on 1st October 1974 although it passed to Gilbert Brown's transport concern Cumbrian Hauliers Ltd when some four years old. Gilbert recalls that both his Mark 1 Marathons (the second was 'Lakeland Roamer' HCK 201S) were marvellous things - when they were going well. He reckoned he was fortunate in having the AEC trained mechanic David Ainsworth to look after them as they did have their problems. 'Lakeland Logger' is pictured on Whinlatter Pass in March 1986 although it did stay in service until the early '90s. Regular work for it was taking cut timber to Bristol and returning with pulp for Barrow in Furness. Both of Gilbert's sons Iain and Andrew drove this Marathon which at the time of writing is still at Brown's Hawkshead depot in one piece - but only just.

Stuart Ritchie admits he was responsible for persuading his father Colin to buy their first Marathon: 'We were running AECs but the Marathon had a lot more about it than the Ergomatic AEC Mandators of the time,' he recalled. Ritchies paid £11,770 in total for the 4x2 unit and a pair of Crane Fruehauf 40' flats, the outfit going onto delivery work for Hills Doors. As JPT 848N was Ritchie's first artic, it's first driver - Malcolm Carr - had to go for a Class 1 test as, like Ritchies other HGV drivers, he only had a Class 3 rigid licence. Malcolm has just celebrated 25 years at Ritchies while the Marathon only lasted a troublesome five years. The TL12 engine was repaired so many times, apparently it never went out of warranty. Ritchies should have been aware that the truck was going to be a problem as even before it was painted when new, it caught fire in the yard. When it was going well, Stuart reckoned nothing would catch it: 'We both loved it and hated it - at the same time,' he said. It returned 7.8mpg, which was very credible in its time.

A modest paint job and a set of trade plates indicates a manufacturers test vehicle although the giveaway that this Marathon was very much a one off is the grille mounted word of Turbine. The vehicle was fitted with the Mark 2 version of Leyland's 2S/350R Gas Turbine engine. The Turbine project was best know for producing a small batch of Ergomatic cab'd 6x4 units, three of which did operational trials with Esso, Burmah Castrol and Shell Mex-BP. While none of these vehicles are believed to have survived, this Marathon is apparently in storage at Coventry Museum. One of the main factors counting against the Turbine vehicles was their poor fuel consumption although the Marathon's early returns were around 5.8mpg.

Top of the Marathon range was the 6x4 unit plated for 44 tonnes gross operation. In this form either the Rolls Royce Eagle 320 or the Cummins NTC 335 were the preferred engine options. This Pickfords example was pictured by Peter Lee coupled to a King step frame extendable semi-trailer. The first Marathon to be built - WTJ 120L - was actually a six wheeler and prior to going to the heavy haulage concern of Tony Morgan, it was used as a long term demonstration vehicle. One of its more interesting hauls was a 7,800 mile round trip to Teheran and back in early 1975. AEC test driver Dick Rivers was accompanied by Jeff Riggins of Asian Transport on this trip. The crew were apparently well impressed with the Marathon's performance in horrendous weather and driving conditions.

P&O Road Services put a batch of 11 day cab'd Marathons into service during 1976 based in South Wales and running in the livery of Coastal Roadways. In standard guise - without the illuminated headboard - the Marathon roof was 9'11" off the ground although it was an easy climb into the cab. While badged as a Leyland, the Marathon's standard TL12 engine was developed by a team under Keith Roberts at the AEC plant in Southall. A lot of this vehicle's production was down at AEC's although it was also built at the Guy Motors factory in Wolverhampton and at the Scammell plant in Watford.

Marathon enthusiasts in the UK had to live on sightings of 4x2 tractor units as spotting any other model was a rare occurrence. However, because the range was exported to all the Leyland markets there was a better chance of seeing something different if you travelled overseas. Seeing an eight wheeled rigid (right) in September '91 in Cyprus was something special as - sadly - that configuration never figured in Leyland's original plans. Some of the Mediterranean islands are a haven for UK second hand exports as in June '89, the six wheeled flat (middle right) was photographed on the island of Gozo (close to Malta). The heavyweight six wheeled tipper (bottom right) was seen in northern France in June '91.

British Steel driver Alan Graham recalls that the Rotherham works of Templeborough and Aldwarke operated a total of 27 Marathons between them from 1976 to the end of 1988. Originally plated at 32 tons gross, these units stayed at this mark even though many Marathons were later uprated for 38 tonnes operation. Fleet number 38 is pictured by driver/photographer Mel Cook in 1986 prior to being unloaded at Gloucester. Like all the Rotherham Marathons this vehicle was double shifted with Trev Middleton being Mel's opposite number. All the company drivers spoke highly of the Marathon's commanding driving position - 'It's never been bettered,' said Alan Graham - as well as the sparkling performance. Alan recalls his vehicle being referred to on the CB as 'A Michael Edwards Rocket' (Michael Edwards being the head of Leyland at the time) while Trev might tell you the story of how two police offices argued about how close Rotherham was to the Midlands. They just couldn't believe how little time he'd taken to cover the distance.

John Starkey set up in haulage during the mid 1950s and because he based his operations next door to the Leyland agency of Brownhills Motor Sales (a company owned by his cousin Ralph Ferry) that was the marque he favoured. John died prematurely in 1977 and XNX 600S was a well liked Marathon bought new by his son Paul who initially took over the running of the business. Paul's brother Bob is behind the wheel while the artic's loaded with Ford engine castings, a regular overnight traffic from Lye near Dudley to Basildon. Starkeys ran about six Marathons (RFD 540R was their first new one) and as the badging suggests, 'The Pride of Brownhills' - and Bob Starkey - regularly went to France and Belgium. John Starkey Transport was bought by Eva Industries although in 1999, Paul Starkey was operating a 17 strong fleet based at Chasetown.

North Yorkshire based John Kettlewell, who now trades as Kirkby Fleetham Haulage Ltd, recalls operating seven or eight sleeper cab fitted Marathons on long distance bulk haulage work during the late '70s and early '80s. Apart from rust breaking out, John reckoned they gave him very little problem and described them as being good workers. Pictured in 1985, AAJ 88T was one of the last in service and usually driven by Allan Richards. It was the only one to be converted with a Primrose third axle with 38 tonnes operation in mind. The vehicle was later sold to Darlington owner driver Keith Tinkler who ran it for another four to five years.

In the early 1980s, Aspatria based Harry & Linda Shanklin only operated this Leyland Marathon although they still preferred to employ a driver for it. In 1980, Ian Holliday had just passed his HGV Class 1 but he was given the chance of the drive and recalls a couple of happy years with the Marathon. Traffic was generally long distance and varied between containers from Felixstowe to Scotland, potato work or even hauling christmas trees. Ian agreed with many other Marathon drivers that the vehicle went really well.

Manufactured in 1981, LHG 166X was one of the last Marathon 2s to be built at the Scammell plant in Watford and wasn't sold until 1982. Bought by Rawcliffes of Mawdesley in Lancashire, it did over 363,000kms in its first two years before being sold for £10,000 to Keith and Philip Iddon during June 1984. The Cummins 290 powered unit gave this Leyland haulier another 10 good years of service (covering over a million kilometres) although not without the odd moment. In 1986, an electrical fire which started in the steering column saw the tractor burnt out. Although written off by the insurance company, the haulier spent three months getting it back to as new condition. Problems in getting spares during the early '90s saw fleet engineer Gary Westby replace the original Leyland rear axle with a Rockwell one which started life in a Seddon Atkinson. The Marathon also sported a Volvo F6 fuel tank and ERF throttle pedal and linkage. The vehicle was cut up for scrap in 1995.

FORD TRANSCONTINENTAL

In the early 1970s, Ford decided they wanted a slice of the tall cab, premium long distance truck market which was then in vogue. In fairness, they had never tried to enter this market - in Europe at least - but what they produced was the head turning classic range of Transcontinentals.

The Transco (at first simply called the 'H' Series) offered a choice of four and six wheeled rigids and tractor units with capacities up to 44 tonnes gross combination weight.

The vehicle was intended for international operation and it took on an international form of construction as Ford used 14 litre Cummins engines, Fuller gearboxes, Rockwell axles, Girling twin stop brakes while the cab was of Berliet build. Even the high tensile steel chassis was from the well tried American Ford Louisville.

When it first came out in 1975, the big Ford was found to be a bit too heavy for UK 32 tons work. In many respects it was way ahead of its time but long distance truck drivers who loved something special really took to the Transcontinental.

For the first five years of production, the truck was assembled in Amsterdam although it was destined for a lingering demise. Problems were created over its production costs and with stiffer competition from other European manufactures, its market share began to slip.

When the five year agreement to buy cabs from Berliet came to an end, Ford had the problem in dealing with Renault, Berliet's new owners. Assembly was switched to the Foden plant of Sandbach Engineering but by 1983, the Transco was seeing its last days and production stopped. The big Ford may have gone, but amongst its many fans it will never be forgotten.

Prior to Ford going into full production with the new Transcontinental range, they took the unusual step of placing 12 tractor units with a variety of operators both in Britain and Germany. Silver Roadways - the bulk contracts division of Tate & Lyle Transport - were to buy SMD 571M although in essence it was a long term evaluation vehicle which Ford followed closely in service. Although having a design rating of 40 tons, this vehicle was operated within the 32 tons maximum then in force in Great Britain.

It may sport a 1980 registration but Bob Hedley's much modified Ford was built in 1976. Made to Italian specification in LHD form, it was apparently pulled off the production line and used by Ford on their four year test programme. When auctioned off by the manufacturer, it was bought by Taylor Transport and Bob bought it in June '85. The only thing original with this motor are the chassis, the rear axle and the air tanks - everything else has been changed. The front axle is of Seddon Atkinson make while the second steer (and lift) axle is of FIA make. The 14 litre Cummins engine is currently tuned to produce 400bhp. Pictured by Bill Kirsop in 1998 at Ashford Truckstop (the Hedley operating centre), Bob was then on Middle East work with Astran although in '99 he was working Italy. What Bob and his Ford haven't been involved with isn't worth writing about but if you happen to meet the much travelled pair just mention X ray machine to him and see what he says.

Marjorie Joyce Morris gave her name to her family's first fruit & veg shop but when her husband Leslie (pictured in the sports jacket) took up the wholesale trade, the MJ Morris title was retained. The firm bought this Transcontinental rigid & trailer in the mid '70s both for collections & deliveries because they were let down then by poor service from outside hauliers. Randolph, one of the sons, is seen on the forklift while another son Tony recalls the Ford's tremendous performance, especially on the hills of Yorkshire: 'You never had to change into the lower range of gears with it,' he said. Although the structure of the Morris business was to totally change, in 1999 the family firm were operating a fleet of 30 refrigerated vehicles still delivering fruit & veg produce.

When Eddie Crozier began driving for Hughie Murphy in the late 1970s his employer only had four vehicles. However, Murphy International - based at Broughshane, Co. Antrim - grew to a 50 strong operation as they became the largest operator of the Ford Transcontinental in Northern Ireland. These four photographs were all taken during the '80s by Cumbria based John Curwen who caught up with the distinctive Fords at either Carlisle or Penrith truck stops. This was often the first stop for Eddie who would often spend 4-5 weeks away from home tramping round Europe or even the Middle East. Eddie was a big fan of the big Ford as he reckoned it went well when compared to anything else then on the road. Although meat was the usual outward bound cargo, return traffic varied in the extreme. The worst, so far as Eddie was concerned was hauling cucumbers from Crete to Kent: 'They smelt awful,' he said, 'and I've never been able to stomach a cucumber since.'

Although Pollock of Musselburgh only had the one Transcontinental and it came to the haulier almost by accident, Ian Pollock still says it was a very good vehicle. JSR 102P was new to the small whisky haulier RS Pirnie of Pitlochry. When Pollock bought the assets of this concern in 1976, it's not surprising that when the big Ford was repainted it was named 'Globetrotter'. Regular Pollock driver of this vehicle was the late Tam Cramb. It's recalled he loved this vehicle so much that on the day it was sold - and he had to remove his personal gear from the truck - he actually started to cry.

The Paris to Dakar rally is as tough as you can get but the Ford Transcontinental made it's mark in a big way on the 1981 run. Lasting between January 1st and the 20th, the event covered 10,000kms (including a crossing of the Sahara Desert) and only three trucks were to finish. This specially converted HA 5035 6x4 articulated tractor unit was to be the first regular series production truck to cross the finishing line.

Tony Van Hee reckoned the Transcontinental was simply way ahead of its time both for power and specification. His Tyneside based concern had 15 of these big Fords (OBB562R was one of their first) primarily to work the Middle East run. Van Hees also operated five Crane Fruehauf tippers with high grade coke being a regular traffic between Hull and Tyneside. Jim Goodrum and Ronnie Tailford were the usual drivers of YTN 593V which is pictured by Andrew Burton at Horton Quarry near Skipton. While being a big fan of the Ford, Tony admitted it wasn't perfect. The wiring, radiator and fuel tanks were some of the ancillaries he recalled as being disasters.

When Midlands BRS won a large contract with the Ford Motor Company, it was virtually anticipated they would buy a number of Ford Transcontinentals - which they did. The just in time collection from a large number of Ford's suppliers were orchestrated from BRS's Bromford Road office in Birmingham although many parts of the BRS network were involved. The deliveries to a number of Ford plants also included a cross channel service serving the Ford factory in Belgium. EJO 184Y was photographed by John Curwen on the M1 during 1986. Other Midlands BRS Transcontinentals included EJO 185Y, ROK 900, 904 and 909Y. In mid '99, the remnants of 184Y were in Hegarty's scrapyard, Toomebridge, Northern Ireland.

BNFL of Sellafield had at least two Transcontinentals (WHH 381Y was another) which were used on general haulage work around the UK. This Mike Parker photograph was taken in April '85. In the mid '80s, BNFL drivers were all in a pool and weren't allocated a specific vehicle. Sid Bushby who drove at the time (he's now a company foreman) recalls his days on the big Ford with mixed emotions: 'They were certainly a powerful machine,' he said, 'but the roads round West Cumbria didn't suit the cab suspension and the swaying could make me sea sick. I'm only 5' 6" and these felt so big. If I wasn't careful when getting out, I'd literally fall out the cab.'

The Transcontinental found itself used by a variety of operators for a variety of jobs - and photographed by a variety of people. This page's compilation is by Pete Jones, Bill Reid and John Curwen, the one face in shot being that of a young David Curwen on a rare day out to London - which was obviously spent spotting Transcontinentals. In many respects, the big Ford was a superb machine. Twin stop brakes was something of a rarity amongst any other truck manufacturer while the form of cab suspension and the use of headlight wipers was not something the mid 1970s had ever seen before. The high rise cab could actually be fitted with a third passenger seat while double bunks were also an option.

BIGGER CABS, BIGGER ENGINES, JUST BIGGER

The biggest and the best is sometimes difficult to gauge as vehicles in general have gradually increased in size. Sleepers have become the norm for many general haulage operations - especially for articulated tractor units - so King of the Road in this domain is having a bigger cab than anyone else.

The heavy haulage crews of old were better off than some for as early as the mid '50s the big Scammells often had huge crew cabs. For general haulage, it wasn't until 1979 that Volvo unveiled their first 'Globetrotter'. As the name suggests, the high top cab was intended to give the international driver far more living space on his long trips away. But such was the demand, by 1983 Volvo were offering this cab on the smaller F10s as well.

Other manufacturers eventually followed this trend using names like Space Cab, Top Line and Roadhaus although the European sleepers are still fairly modest when compared to those in use in the USA.

As the trend for longer hauls at heavier weights has been coupled to the need for quicker journey times, it created the demand for bigger engines. Identifying the Supertrucks of the '90s meant you may have to read the small numbers on the cab doors denoting either engine size or output.

In 1958, the latest Gardner 6LX-150 was felt to produce more than enough power for 24 tons. In the 1990s, such an output would only suit a standard 7.5 tonner. The imports of the '60s changed this emphasis overnight and as the decades have passed, the standards of engine power has gradually increased.

As the maximum weights for UK general haulage artics reached 40/41 tonnes in the late 1990s, then 400bhp has become the norm. Having a truck with an engine above the standard is how special status is obtained.

They may not have the most imaginative paint job, but so far as big engines are concerned then the British Army's Rolls Royce CV12TCE powered Scammell Commanders are as big as you can get. There's 26.108 litres of engine capacity hidden under the bonnet although it's modestly tuned to produce 'only' 625bhp at 2,100rpm. Ready for installation, the engine alone tips the scales at 4,386lbs (almost 2 tons). This engine was chosen - in preference to the Cummins KTA 600 - to standardise with the engine of the Challenger battle tanks which are it's regular load. With a Scammell rating of 101.4 tonnes, the Commanders were built to hold a road speed of 40mph - loaded or empty. The first eight (of 125) Commanders went into service during March and April 1984 and while they've given the military excellent service, the question being asked - as the 21st century approaches - is what will replace this ageing Supertruck.

Opposite and above:- To many drivers, both here and abroad, having a Scania with a V8 engine made you the real King of the Road - and going by the Swedish photograph, the English expression also had an International meaning. For David Laidlow, it was more a case of necessity as the roads in northern Scotland are particularly harsh on any modestly powered trucks. Although his HQ was in Orkney, his six V8 Scanias tended to work out of Scrabster. Driver Gary Miller recalls the first 142 was NBS 832Y although NBS 974Y had an extra luxury cab. Gary had the 141 TNS 870W before getting the brand new 142 C196 RBS in November '85. The pictured box van was generally used to carry whisky from the two island distilleries to Dumbarton although in contrast, regular loads back to Orkney - on flat trailers - were barrels of aviation fuel. David Laidlow sold out to Sutherlands in the late '80s but then set up a ferry service from Invergordon to Orkney.

Seen across Whitby harbour in April 1992, there doesn't seem anything special to the Volvo 38 tonner loading up with 400 bags of shellfish. Look closer and you'll spot the chrome surround to the black grille, an immediate indicator of the F16. Although most F16s come with the Globetrotter cab, this was one of two with the standard cab that apparently went new to Metcalfes of Penrith - the 470 number plate denoting the engine's horsepower. John Twiname bought the 1988 unit when about 18 months old and named it 'Monarch of the Glen.' When asked in May '99, John said he was well pleased with the F16 which was still in service. He reckoned it was always well on top of the job - even with more than 1.5 million kilometres behind it. The F16 still had the original engine, gearbox & back axle while fuel returns, with a flat trailer, were said to be 7-7.5mpg.

Sandy Morton recalled it was something of a treat when he bought this F16 in 1989: 'I just have an ordinary car,' he reasoned, 'so I thought I'd buy myself a good motor to work with.' He was unable to drive the big Volvo for much more than a year as expansion plans encouraged him to expand his forestry work. In 1999 he was operating a five strong fleet of Volvos and the F16 was still in service having covered something like 1 million miles. In its time it's been double shifted and Sandy reckons he's never had any problems finding someone to drive this motor: 'They'll come off a new FH to drive the F16,' he says, 'it's such a good goer.' The owner reckons it's also reasonable on fuel - better than his FH12s, he says.

H554 EKP was something pretty special as it was the first factory built eight wheeled Volvo F16 heavy hauler to come to the UK. New to Cliffe Plant of Rochester, it had a strange and quiet early life. Apparently it was badly damaged in an accident before passing to HE Services of Strood although when it came north to Heanor in late '97, it had covered very little mileage. This Rod Spratley photograph taken near Chester shows driver Jason Yates with a 153' long, 96 tonne cold box which was heading from Acrefair to Ellesmere Port. The two mates on this job were Wayne Upfold and George Duncan. While it's always difficult to rate the strength of any heavy haulage tractor, Jason says this F16 has hauled 300 tonnes - unassisted - when moving a transformer near Leith.

It may be something of a coincidence that not long after the Scammell plant at Watford was closed (following the Leyland Daf merger) that an eight wheeled heavy haulage version of the 95.380 was produced. A double flitched, wider and deeper 6x4 chassis was converted by GINAF Trucks adopting its hydropneumatic suspension system for the 8x4. The vehicle was actually developed from eight wheelers built for the Israel market. The first of about 15 sold in the UK was G630 MGG (destined for Cadzow Heavy Haulage) and it appeared at the IRTE Show at Telford in May 1989. Although Leyland Daf bannered these vehicles as fit for 200 tonnes GCW, concern with gearing meant some 8x4s - without torque convertors - were only rated for 150 tonnes gross operation. G380 ONN may have started life with Hills of Pyebridge but within three years it had joined the Space Cab G815 GAB at Allellys. Ken Colley drove this latter vehicle when new and while moving rail locomotives is routine for this Warwickshire based concern, 4472 - The Flying Scotsman - was always a bit special.

Heavy haulage photographer Dennis Tomlin recalled that on Sunday 14th December 1986 the early morning light wasn't at its best. However, obtaining police permission to walk along the closed section of the M53, he recorded this moment of heavy hauling history. Will we ever see five such heavy haulage tractors (a Scammell S24, three Scammell Contractors and a Nicolas Tractomas) in a situation like this again combining to move 1,200 tonnes gross. Although the haul between Ellesmere Port and Shell's Stanlow refinery was only about five and half miles, Dennis said that half way down the motorway the load stopped so the Econofreight crew could take refreshments.

The Italians aren't generally interested with expensive liveries, instead they allow the manufacturers markings to speak for themselves. Mercedes (and MAN) have long used a model coding system where the first two numbers - 19 in this case - indicate the vehicle's gross weight in tonnes, while the last two letters indicate the engine's size - 480bhp. In July 1992, this black Merc stood head and shoulders above many others in sheer engine size alone. The vehicle had just been bought by very good friend Nicky Armstrong who although originating from the UK has spent most of his working life based at Aosta in Northern Italy. Nicky and the 1948 spent six years together on traction work criss crossing the

Continent. The tractor proved itself particularly quick up the hills provided it didn't get stuck behind something like a Mercedes 1629. This latter vehicle, according to its driver, could actually claim to be the slowest truck up Mont Blanc.

In many people's eyes, the Iveco Eurotech is just another fleet motor. Where it has made friends is with its medium and highroof cab options. Drivers who've spent many nights in much smaller sleepers highly rate the extra space the Eurotech provides. Containerships UK - based on Teesside - have bought around 60 of these vehicles through North East Truck & Van. Strangely, a lot of these currently operate in Russia (the fleet based in St Petersburg is around the 90 mark). The privately owned parent concern of Containerships was set up in Finland during 1968. The company now specialises in a door to door service from anywhere in the UK across to most parts of northern Europe & Russia.

When it comes to sleeper cabs, you don't get much bigger than what's on the American market. This is slightly ironic because anyone who's driven a conventional Peterbilt, Kenworth, Mack or the like will be aware, their standard cabs are close to claustrophobic. One Brit who's had his hands on more American trucks than many is John Scholey. Seen on the back of the curtainsider, John may come from East Yorkshire but his vehicles are normally registered through his base in Holland. The

Kenworth WB900 was new in 1985 to Nilriah Equipment of Fort Lauderdale. This top of the range Liberty model (it had every additional extra available) used to haul luxury yachts between Florida and California. The Kenworth built sleeper pod is a 60" - the measurement of its length along the chassis. John ran it from 1995 until 1998 and then sold it to the Three Ring American Circus.

SUPER TRUCKS OF THE '90s

Like many in the industry, Philip Henson hadn't seen anything quite like the Magnum: 'As soon as I saw it on test in France,' he recalled, 'I decided to have one. It wasn't a case of Renault wanting to sell me one, I wanted to buy it.' As Chairman of Patricks of Kettering (a company set up by his Great Uncle Stephen Patrick in 1878) Philip has seen the transition from traders in leather products, to International haulier. Since Philip did the first run to Florence in 1967 with an 'F' reg Ford Transit van, Patricks have become an Italian specialist and now have a fleet of 17 including two vehicles based at Brescia. The Magnum (complete with body) cost £54,000 and gave the haulier reasonable service: 'No one liked to reverse with it,' said Philip. It was sold in 1997.

Although Alec & Pat Grant's Norfrost fleet are dominated by Scania, it's not surprising when Renault announced the Magnum the Grants wanted one as a company flagship as at the time, they also had a Renault car dealership in Thurso. J132HSK was apparently the first Magnum in Scotland (one chassis number ahead of Robin Borthwick's) and had the 500 V8 Mack engine. Gary Miller ('Wild Rover' was his CB handle) drove this vehicle for some 16 months when he was based at the Norfrost Perth depot and felt it was slightly overated - when compared to the big V8 Scanias. The clutch thrust bearing also gave bother as it used to pop out, although after the engine was accidentally cooked (when ran short of water) the subsequent overhaul dramatically enhanced its performance. It was later sold to an owner driver in England.

Bewick Transport were big Scania users but when boss Dennis Smith began the International division, he decided to look at other makes. Company driver Andrew Armistead had a Magnum demonstrator for a week and because he was so impressed, Bewicks ordered two of the 420 powered units. Pictured by Dave Weston at the Milnthorpe HQ in Cumbria, the units were first driven by Micky Brown and Eddie Potts. The International vehicles usually do a round trip a week between Cumbria and Germany or the Benelux countries. The Bewick fleet was subsequently absorbed into the WRM Logistics concern.

A15 POG started life in Scotland in 1992 as a 4x2 Magnum tractor unit. Perry's of Gobowen were to transform the vehicle when it was stretched, transplanted with the double drive rear bogie of a Foden eight wheeler and appended with a hydraulic lift 'pusher' axle. Clive Heathcock set up the commercial repair business (they're also a Renault service dealer) in 1962, the Perry name coming from the origins of the River Perry which is behind the garage. Clive has since been joined by his son Glynne who was driving the Magnum when pictured by Dave Weston on the A5. The eight wheeler stands at 21 tonnes unladen and is equipped with Heathcock built wrecking gear.

John David Riby set up in haulage about 1981 and although he once ran ERFs, his fleet is now the largest Magnum operator in Yorkshire. In July '99 their 23rd Magnum (supplied by Thompson Commercials) had just been delivered, their first one being P839 NKH. Dave Riby took to the big Renault as a way of enhancing his company's image as well as giving his driving staff an ideal truck to live in. As European haulage is a company speciality, the Riby drivers can be away for up to four weeks a time. The Hull - Zeebrugge route is the usual way across the North Sea and pictured leaving the ferry is P861 UKH which had Paul Schartad as its first regular driver.

You could say: 'The King is dead - Long live the Kin
With Econofreight selling the ex Sunters Tractomas to
operator in East Africa, the mantle of Heavy Haulage Ki
has been taken up by their distinctive 6x6 Unipower. Se
on Teesside during July '99, this 150' long vessel w
moved into ICI Wilton from the Tees Offshore Base. Ga
Porter is sitting in the Volvo F10 design of cab while
brother Paul is on walkabout. Hardest job was that
John Gordon who as trailer steersman was sat at the re
balancing the vessel on its three point suspension. All
weight was around 279 tonnes and ensuring it had an ea

o hour ride were Constables Stuart Fawcett and Steve
glestone although the walking pace hardly tested their
nda Pan European motor cycles. What did keep the
ers awake was the shattering bellow every time the
mmins engine electronic fan cut in. Unipower desig-
ted this vehicle as a 'C' type which is a reference to the
l Scammell ranges of Constructor and Contractor. Only
ee vehicles of this type have been built. The
onofreight vehicle was the prototype, a 6x6 oilfield
ck went to Indonesia while a 6x4 tractor was sold into
kistan.

Volvo announced their head turning FH12 range in 1993 as a replacement for the F10/12. At the heart of this stylish vehicle was a new 12 litre engine producing 340, 380 or 420bhp. It was apparently only available as a four or six wheeled rigid / tractor unit. Some heavy haulage operators did opt for an eight wheeled conversion of the FH 6x4 but so far as UK general hauliers were concerned, their only choice (until the FM range was announced in late '98) was between an FL7 or an FL10. For them, the FH12 eight wheeled rigid just didn't exist, however, as seen in Northern France during June 1997, there was such a vehicle in production.

Any truck driver who knows the testing A9 road north of Tain will be aware of why Stevens of Wick opt for a powerful fleet line up. Five of these FH16-470 Globetrotters were operated - four 'L' reg and one on 'M' plate. To ensure the loads of fish landed at Scrabster can quickly reach the regular delivery points of North Shields, Grimsby and Fleetwood, the company operates a system of jump jockeys where one driver moves between different vehicles to increase the legal running time of the outfit. It's not unknown for one 'jockey' to drive four different trucks in one day. When you're double manning in this - or conventional form - the Globetrotter cab makes the job a lot easier.

The Scania 143 was to win a lot of friends including Lorn Freight of Fraserburgh as up until 1992, the company had been Volvo users. Established in 1978 by husband & wife Alfred and Lorna Eddie, the Lorn Freight title was used to avoid any confusion with Alfred's brother, Arthur Eddie, who ran a similar haulage operation in the town. In mid 1999, Lorn were operating three V8 powered Scanias, the third being N140 VSS, a second 143-450. Derek McLeod and Richard Simmers are the current drivers of the pictured 144 and 143. The company specialises in Continental fridge haulage usually hauling fish to wholesale and canning factory outlets.

To celebrate 50 years in haulage, John Thomas - MD of the company his father set up in 1948 - put what's known as 'The Gold Lorry' on the road. As the variety of slogans on the trailer curtains suggest, a large number of suppliers either gave donations, parts free of charge for this outfit or gave Thomas' a substantial discount. In total more than £20,800 was raised (the figure's still growing) while all these monies have gone to the local Macmillan Cancer Centre. The one big problem with S50 KTL is when it comes to routine trailer changes: 'We try and keep the combination together as much as possible,' said John, 'because the Scania 124-400 Topline doesn't look right pulling one of our normal trailers - and the gold trailer doesn't look right behind one of our normal units.'

The Four Series Scania had a lot to live up to after it was launched in 1995 although it quickly picked up the title of International Truck of the Year in 1996. Top of the range was to be the 530bhp version of its 14 litre engine and in July '99, the James McHugh fleet had three of these well liked units in service. Based at Londonderry in Northern Ireland, the company was established in 1968. The current owner is Kevin McGlinchey whose 22 strong fleet (19 of which are Scania) are worked on international traffic.

As soon as the T Cab Scania was unveiled, it certainly created attention. Although Kevin Dalgarno of KD Offshore (Southampton) Ltd operated a high profile fleet of specialist Volvo tankers, he felt the T cab would create the right visual impact when seen alongside cruise liners like the QEII. Established in 1994, the company manages marine waste and their treatment works at Marchwood is described as the largest marine waste facility in the UK. The T124LA 6x2 NA400 tractor unit is regularly driven by long serving driver Del Healey. Although he drove a Volvo FH prior to the Scania arriving, he describes his new truck as 'excellent'.

S6 PSL was the last of six Leyland Daf Space Cab XF-480s Pollocks put into service during August 1998. A year later, the Pollock fleet was approaching the 80 mark and although all manner of supertrucks are in service, these were the first Dafs bought by the company since the mid '80s. Named 'My Way', in tribute to the late Frank Sinatra, the XF normally has Ian Newton as its driver. Individual names have been a Pollock trademark for many years although since 1992, the imprint 'Simply The Best' has become another trademark. Although it's intended as a retort to a local competitor, few transport enthusiasts would disagree with such an observation.

Some operators feel that investment in the latest generation of Supertruck with a 500+bhp engine will naturally produce bigger fuel use. The Fehrenkotter concern based at Sassenburg near Munster, Germany don't necessarily agree as their latest 2553 Actros is returning the best fuel returns in their 60 strong fleet. In fairness, the crew of this vehicle - husband & wife team Wladislav and Marianna Niescioruk - are a bit special. They've been with the company for 20 years and cover something like 200,000kms each year. Like the rest of the fleet, the crew get a new vehicle every five years but to reward their excellent driving technique, their latest Mercedes was this top of the range model.

This Mercedes Actros 2548 Space Cab was taken into service by Robert Summers during March '99. It's photographed by Gary Paton at his regular spot in Bothwell Services on the M74. Robert Summers set up in haulage with his wife Sally during 1970 although in '99, their son David ran the 26 strong fleet. The first Summers vehicle was a second hand Leyland Super Comet but the company took to Mercedes after buying a small 508 in 1978. 'Kingdom Concorde' - enroute to Heathrow - is pictured with Jim Gear at the wheel although Angus Mitchell was its regular day driver. The Summers vehicles' individual names are prefixed 'Kingdom' - as the company is located in the Kingdom of Fife - then suffixed with aircraft names, as a link to the nearby RAF Leuchars.

Supertrucks don't come more special than R57 KSA. F&J Gilbert (Francie and his son James) have been in business based at Kintore in north east Scotland since 1989. Although Francie's previous Mercedes 1850 was a bit special, his latest Mega Space Cab Actros 1857 was first of its kind - north of the border - when new on 1st August 1997. Coupled to a Gray & Adams van, the combination's price tag was around £120,000 as the Mercedes sports extras like air conditioning, alloy super singles and a full aerodynamic kit. Although Francie did run to Italy for eight years, the BSE crisis ended these trips away. In mid '99 his normal delivery pattern involved 35-40 shop deliveries of hanging Scottish beef starting at Doncaster and ending at Great Yarmouth.